Also by Oli Hille

Trading for Profit

*Internet Marketing - For Income,
Influence and Impact*

*Social Media - For Income,
Influence and Impact*

*How to Become an Amazon #1
Bestselling Author - and Make Money!*

Science Fiction Short Stories

Visit the author's website:
www.LifestyleBook.com

See all books by the author:
www.Amazon.com/author/1

Creating the Perfect Lifestyle

Amazon #1 Bestseller

First Edition

Published by: Empire Publishers

ISBN: 978-0-473-21508-8

Dedicated to my three beautiful children:

Bleuette, Toby and Christian.

I hope and pray you enjoy an abundant
Lifestyle filled with passion,
love, joy and abundance.

Thank you to my lovely wife Fleur who put up
with me before I made changes to improve
our Lifestyle, and who still does.

Thank you to my "Inner Circle"
– you know who you are.

Thank you to my editor Virlane Torbit.

Book Reviews

"Creating the Perfect Lifestyle is the must have book of the century. Its helpful advice can set you on the pathway of living the life you were meant to live. By far this is one of the most interesting titles this reviewer has ever discovered. Oli Hille should stand up and take a bow, he has written a book that can literally change the way you live your life."
Suzie Housley, Reviewer - Midwest Book Review (USA)

"This book is a must. It is a game changer. Over the last 2 years I have read just under 200 books on self help, psychology and business. Oli's book is the central station of all great things included. You will be amazed at the golden nuggets you will discover in this phenomenal book. Seriously, buy it now."
Dr Anthony Close

"If you only intend to read one book this year; make it this one!"
Graham White

"Absolutely brilliant and important work that everyone should read. It is one of things you read and just go, why has no-one told me this before?"
James Gurnsey

"I thought I was hooked on Facebook.....until I started reading this book! I have not been online for a few days, because I cannot stop reading it! Amazing and insightful!"
Yvonne VanNiel

"A must read book."
Nira Ranasinghe

"This is the first review I've written on Amazon. I had to do it because Oli Hille's book is amazing. This is a must read book to be placed at the top of the list of books to read."
Laurie Brantley

"I wish I had read a book like this when I was a teenager. They should put it in the school curriculum."
Andy Chapman

"Oli explains how to create more time in your day, more money in your pocket, more contentment in life and so much more. Oli Hille has become my favorite contemporary author."
Laurie S

"This is a great book - I've already learned a huge amount. It's written in a really clear, readable style, which made it easy to approach difficult subjects I've often shied away from. I have to say that it's how to create a great life anywhere in the world!"
Christopher Howard

"I have been calling "Creating the Perfect Lifestyle" a book, but it's so much more. It is a reference that you are going to want to keep handy and refer to again and again. The only drawback is that it wasn't released years ago. "Creating the Perfect Lifestyle" has helped me immensely. I can't help but think how nice it would have been to learn all of this when I was twenty!"
Tracy Morrow

"A great read with absolute honesty and inspiration intertwined throughout. It is a must read for anyone looking to re-focus their life and re-set personal and financial goals for their own success."
Jason Stephens

"Great read!! Very informative and enjoyable with many practical solutions you can implement today! It's not often you get so much quality information backed up research in one place. Well worth reading!"
Samuel Kerr

"I love this book! It is written in a simple yet powerful language. And it works!"
Vladimir Astrakhan

"I have to say that out of all the books I read last year and since this year begun, Oli's "Creating the Perfect Lifestyle", is the best book that all people in the world should read."
Washington Junior

"This book quickly gets to the heart of how to create the perfect lifestyle for YOU. Each of us is different, yet with these easy, tried-and-true steps one really can get to a point where you say - "YES this is my life and I love it!" I am living that life right now by putting into practice the practical steps that Oli has outlined. You won't be disappointed."
Catlin V

"I feel very fortunate to have access to "Creating the Perfect Lifestyle" and I wanted to make sure those I cared about did too; the nicest feedback I can give is that I was excited to buy copies to a lot of friends as a small sign of appreciation!"
Foundations of Success

"Oli Hille has written one of the best books on how to live the life of your dreams, thanks a million Oli. This book contains all the big stuff and all the little stuff you will ever need to know."
Sapphire Roae Kaahu

"Yes, this is absolutely the kind of book I wish someone had given me forty years ago ... or even thirty years ago ... or twenty years ago ... heck, I would've settled for this five years ago! I know that I'm emailing a link to all of my friends and family right after I post this review. And, for the record, I'll be happy to pay the price for any in my close circle!"
Edward Lee

"Every 40 or 50 years, a book is written, quite frankly, for its author's generation.... Mr Hille has taken the age old "Secrets of a Perfect Lifestyle" and translated them into our times...and convincingly. While I am not acquainted with the author, I wish I were. You nailed it Sir!!"
David Rodwell

"Oli is a true inspiration in his new book he outlines setting your goals among other things, I set my goals and not stopping until I succeed. I saw him go to # 1 on Amazon. He is a humble generous man and I recommend his book to everyone."
Lisa Young

"Every now and then you stumble upon an author/book that you can't put down, more rarely do stumble upon one who with his work manages to Inspire and Motivate like Oli Hille. This is truly one I cannot put down and when I do I am constantly inspired by Oli's work to find more time and get things done. I have changed so many things in my life since buying this book and I want to thank Oli personally for getting me back on track to live my life fully."
Anne Brisbane

"This book was an amazing read. A must read and more importantly "A must Practice" book!"
Larry Purchase

"I loved loved loved this little gem of a book which is seriously the best value on Amazon today. If you're serious about designing a new lifestyle for yourself, Oli has gone above and beyond to give you every single tool you'll need to do that."
M. Gray

"My wise-beyond-years granddaughter recently noted that she wouldn't read a book to the end if it didn't grab her heart and mind in the first chapter; I am confident she would make it to the final page of the Creating the Perfect Lifestyle."
Anna Weber

"This book is simply amazing! You must check this book out! I would give this book 10 stars if that were possible. I would recommend this as a very best title in the entire field of self-improvement, because is very easy and useful read, enjoyable and extremely helpful. The tips and guidelines in the book are simple easy to follow, and will amaze you."
Mihaela C.

"This book is terrific! I sent it to my three children as Christmas gifts and they also appreciate the wisdom therein. Couldn't recommend it more highly."
Jenifer Alexander

"It's a must-have for anyone who has had enough of just getting by; for those who are ready to start living their dreams, aka their 'perfect lifestyle'. Thumbs up!"
Kim Chernecky

"This is the best Lifestyle book I've ever read and I can thoroughly recommend it to everyone who is interested in achieving his or her full potential in life."
Verica Martin

"Thanks to your book Oli I completely reassessed my path in life and realized that I needed to change my high stress corporate life for one that was in synergy with my personal beliefs."
Tina Emsden

"Have you ever thought of all the common sense advice you collect in a lifetime, and wish you could present it as gift to you children? Oli's done it for us."
David French

"You have written a very highly motivational life changing book. It has made a huge difference in my lifestyle, even though I'm taking baby steps to get there... I'm pushing forward to the perfect lifestyle, thanks to you."
Ginger Pierce

"Oli's book transports you from the plane of existence to the plane of living! A simple yet powerful guide to questioning the status quo and recreating your lifestyle to lead an authentic, fulfilling life!"
KV Dipu

"Creating the Perfect Lifestyle is a must read for all people that do not wish to live their life passively and reactively."
Leila Ira

"One of the most empowering books I have read so far on Lifestyle and success. Oli Hille, is really a great writer. I kept on reading over and over again. A must read book."
Kelvin Kline

"Fantastic amalgamation of the best published books, with Oli's personal observations and beliefs."
Catherine Cale-Roberts

"It is very rare to have a book that caters to all areas of your life be it economical, relational, spiritual, physical, mental and emotional. Creating the Perfect Lifestyle does just that; the author helps you discover what your inner desires are and gives you a step by step guide on refining it and putting it in to action. CTPL has changed the way I look at earning money and has empowered me to not settle for less than I can be. It is user friendly and very straight to the point."
Michael Blissett

"Creating the Perfect Lifestyle is one of the best inspirational, motivational books I've ever read. So honest, and straight to the point. You can tell the author's unselfish desire for helping his readers put everything they read from his book into action."
Maria Carbon

"This is the best book I have read in forever!! I was very pleased with the book. It really addresses motivation which I lack and that has been a big help for me. I have now started writing the book I have put off for so long!!"
Teena Adams

"What an amazing book, what more can I say! This book literally rejuvenated me and instilled that hope in me that sometimes gets forgotten when dealing with daily life."
CeCe

"Creating the Perfect Lifestyle is the best inspirational book I've ever read... wisely written, shows you the tools and steps to start planning the life you've wished before. This book must be spread worldwide! I'm on the way of creating my own and perfect lifestyle. It really shook me!"
Julio Canas

"Great Book, I just started reading and setting my Goals - (this week). Something I have not done in my life. I am inspired to create my Perfect Lifestyle. Thank you."
Willow

"I feel happy and won't stop in dreaming BIG. Good book, worth to read and re-read. :)"
Dorota

"I found "Creating the Perfect Lifestyle", a really great book! It is very good value for money and very easy to read and absorb the information. I enjoyed Oli's book very much and felt inspired to finish my own children's picture book."
Catherine Muir

"What it does do is make the concepts truly accessible and obtainable! How Oli accomplishes this I cannot say, but I feel totally reinvigorated and positive as a result....and that's everything to me!"
Hakinan

"This is an excellent Book to educate and inspire you to improve your life. It is enjoyable to read, and keeps your attention. By giving doable activities, it can really change your life. Well done Oli Hille."
Jenny Paisley

"A great source of valuable info. It's the one book I go back time after time for inspiration. Full of great links to have a better life."
Josef Mueller

"This is one Book that made me feel I have been living my life pensively, it practically brings you to the consciousness of the events around you."
Jewel Fitila

"Creating the Perfect Lifestyle is a gem. Oli Hille clearly presents a plethora of transformational possibilities to empower and forge a new path with life. Creating the Perfect Lifestyle will inspire, infuse and redeem the most precious gift of all, time."
Ron Mazellan

"After reading "Creating the Perfect Lifestyle" I identified where I needed to make changes in my life and learnt that nothing is impossible when you put your mind to it. Thanks Oli for taking to time to make your book so easy to understand and digest and even easier to follow."
Mariska Araba Taylor-Darko

"A seminal work: well constructed, thoughtfully written and offering perspectives that you simply won't find anywhere else. This book clearly comes from someone who has been living an authentic and congruent life. Every adult should read this & give it to their kids."
Ingrid Burling

"This book is a real 'Must have!' Oli is a genuine, energetic, driven guy who is dedicated to life improvement for all. We can all learn so much from his fabulous book! Go buy it now!"
Andy Shepherd, Life Coach

"Great Book, I just started reading and setting my goals - (this week). Something I have not done in my life. I am inspired to Create My Perfect Lifestyle. Thank you."
Williametta Cummings

"People are looking for simple and powerful strategies to move forward in life, Oli Hille's book delivers, pure and simple, a must read!"
Derek Reid

"Oli covers all the topics necessary to create the life you dream of living. Creating the Perfect Lifestyle is outlined in a way that is easy to follow and the information he shares gives you the "cream" of all the topics. You no longer have to sort through media to find answers to lead you to your next step. It's all there! This book makes an inspirational daily book as well as a working plan for your life. As an author, mental health therapist and coach, this would be great for all my clients. Once you buy it, I encourage you to buy a copy for a friend and become sharing and accountability partners."
Candess Campbell

"This book really made me think, and see things differently. Reading it has changed my life. Thank you Oli, keep up the good work."
Zoe Willsdon

"Great book from a great writer who believes in tomorrow. I learned a lot."
Imad Khalaf

"Oli offers inspiring insight to creating the life of your dreams! Read Creating the Perfect Lifestyle so that you too can learn to follow your dreams."
Marisa DiTommaso

"An excellent book, I found the section on goal setting particularly useful. I wish I had read a book like this when I was a teenager. They should put it in the school curriculum. It is just what young people need; practical help to make the most of their opportunities."
Dr Claire McNally

"Oli has a gift for presenting the reader with concise and easy to follow steps, which in my view, can act as a powerful catalyst for change."
Michael Toothill

"I found it helpful and insightful with interesting examples to demonstrate points. I would recommend this as a guide to organizing your finances to anyone."
Jaron McCutcheon

"You can go among the many chapters in this book and craft improvements to your lifestyle. So what I liked best about this book is that it's not a road map but a menu. Pick from the items that appeal to you or speak to you in some way and find ways to improve your life."
Joanne Daneman, Amazon "Top 10" Reviewer

"This book is so easy to read, and has some kick ass tips in there. Are you seriously trying to give away all your secrets?"
Oli Robinson

"A great book about lifestyle, written with style."
Dean Smith

"This is an epic "how to" with depth and simplicity rarely seen today. Get it, read it, give it, do it."
Sam Knight

"What I appreciated most is that it is written in a way the makes you realize you can achieve your dreams, regardless of how little you have to start with."
Vicky Lang

"What would it be like if you could create the absolute perfect life for yourself and include your friends and family in that perfect world. Guess what? You can create exactly what you want. If you can dream it and commit to making it happen, Oli Hille will show you just how to make Your Perfect Lifestyle, a reality!"
Richard Kelley, MD

"A fantastic read that I am sure will provide inspiration for many readers."
Sarah Baxter

"As I read, I became so engrossed in the material he presented and making extensive notes on my personal goals and what I might do to achieve them, that I forgot to make review notes. So I've re-read, and am continuing to learn."
Cassandra Barnes

"I've read quite a few self-improvement books, some good and some bad, but Creating the Perfect Lifestyle stands out from the crowd as being well-written, organized and practical in its approach."
D Buxman, Amazon Top Reviewer

"Creating The Perfect Lifestyle is an excellent book. Anything is possible if I put in the time and effort. This is the message of this uplifting book."
Robert Yokoyama

"Creating the Perfect Lifestyle is a perfect blueprint for life and if you follow its recommendations, you cannot fail to be successful, overcome obstacles and enjoy your journey through life. This book should be on everyone's bookshelf, next to the dictionary and thesaurus."
Verica Peacock

"Oli is one of my favorite motivators! He deeply cares about helping people and, unlike many, has gained his character by persevering through pain. This fact is what makes this book (and his others) so full of Hope."
Clay Nelson

"Creating the Perfect Lifestyle is well written, informative, highly recommendable and helpful to people of all ages - even to this octogenarian. So, thank you Oli."
Godfrey Warren

"I read "Creating the Perfect Lifestyle" and it's definitely made an impact on my attitude. I've made some subtle, yet meaningful changes in my thinking that have made a big, positive difference. Thanks Oli!"
Garth A. Tobler

"This is a great book, full of positivity! Although I've read it all the way through, I still enjoy 'dipping' into it every now and again to get my dose of Lifestyle tips."
Keely Kendrick

"Oli Hille makes a fine friend, a respected tutor, and a guy you'd like to spend time with - because your life is in order and moving the way that pleases you."
Grady Harp, Amazon "Top 10" Reviewer

"With Oli's book you will think beyond yourself, feel beyond yourself, walk beyond yourself."
Roger Aburto

"Oli Hille's book a great addition to the works of author's like Dave Ramsey, Robert Kiyosaki, and Tim Ferriss. He really gets to the core of what makes people truly happy."
Steve Burns

"If you only want to buy one book about this topic, I would definitely recommend this one. You get a wealth of information for your money, it's worth every cent and has the power of changing your life."
Frithjof M

"After 70 years living in the fast track and going through most problems life can dish out -- I find Oli's advice is SPOT ON. Read this book -- IT'S A LIFE CHANGER."
DW Shuker

"Finally, a useful, practical, positive, straightforward book. Oli Hille is living proof of the "I CAN DO" attitude and his belief in us as a progressive, innovative and creative world and people. Thank you Oli for your generosity of heart and mind to share ideas on HOW we can create and live a positive, happy, challenging and satisfying lifestyle."
Emilie Sila'ila'i

"What a fantastic book you have written, good on you in educating people without any finance background. I wish I had read a book like yours when I was younger."
Pranesh Tulsi

"This came to me at the perfect point in my life! It all seems like common sense, yet I would not have had the motivation to think of ways to progress my life without reading this book. The personal examples give the words a voice and a lot of these situations are those which I've been in myself."
Erin Johnston

"As a single parent to two children I feel I never have the time to read books, indeed it feels like a luxury these days! However when I started reading Oliver Hille's Lifestyle book I couldn't put it down!"
Robyn Dodd

"Oli's book it has really inspired me to live on the edge."
Anita Parkinson

"This is a great blueprint for business and life!"
Jason Baudendistel

"Great Book Oli, I loved the chapters on Children and Television. I love the fact that is book is very practical and easy to understand. I think this book has some great keys that will help people to have successful and fulfilling lives well done!!"
Cushla Pretty

"Enjoyed this, well written and entertaining as well as bringing some financial and lifestyle issues into focus."
Ben Jelly

"What a great piece of work! Oli, hats off to you. There is some really useful stuff here. I particularly like the advice of. If you can't buy it now, don't buy it! I've always said 'If you can't afford it with crisp £10 notes, you can't afford it!' Lots of really positive, thought provoking ideas! A warm and honest good luck from me!!"
Nick Moreton

"I intended to have a quick flick through Oli's book but two hours later I was still going! Oli has written a wide ranging, informative and interactive guide that will benefit anyone interested in creating the perfect lifestyle."
Josh Burrell

"In an easy-to-read style, the author has squeezed into one book big life topics such as goals, time, wealth, priorities, property, relationships and others and left the reader with a toolbox of tips that are really helpful."
Luke Buxton

"Very informative with a relaxed and easy to read style. Inspirational ideas which motivated me to look at new opportunities with renewed insight! Well done Oli."
Kirstin O'Brien

"What an enjoyable and interesting read! A lot of practical advice written in a way that even my 16 year old would enjoy, understand and follow. I found this book both inspirational and thought provoking."
Tina Garland

"Thanks for writing the lifestyle book. I like the approach being more holistic than focused too narrowly like many books of this type are. The section on the importance of children I found particularly refreshing."
Ian Gilmour

"This is such an easy and enjoyable read, full of practical and insightful applications for life."
Graeme Newton

"Your Lifestyle book is a fantastic read because you have effectively put together a real-life perspective on the things that matter in life and it covers the important subjects and takes a no-nonsense approach to putting them across. Well done. I will be recommending this book."
Phil Metaxas

"Get out of bed and get started ! Mr Hille's book covers all facets of how to create a lifestyle less ordinary and tells how to have fun doing it."
Graham Parlane

"A very useful and inspiring read, with lots of great practical tips."
Deane Taylor

"Very readable and practical. Interesting, and covered a wider range of topics than I was expecting."
Rachel Hay

"Oli's book should be read by school leavers, business men/woman and anyone thinking big!"
Steve Jeff

"I found Oli Hille's book a very good read and covered a large number of basic truths about wise investment, setting goals and how we can all reach our own 'ultimate' lifestyle. This book should be made available to and read by all young people before they leave school so they know what alternative options could be open to them with a little insight."
Jeremy Head

"Great tips for those who are interested in changing their life style around and going for their passion."
Jeff Rivera

"A great read....found myself on page 25 before I knew it. A well structured and thought through practical book written by someone with real life experience."
Roger Barley

"Oli has a direct and fast paced style that makes for an enjoyable and engrossing read. In the financial chapters the candid examples from his own life are courageous and tend to align the reader more directly with the author. There are spectacular moments like the chapter on children."
Roseann Cameron

"Sometimes these kind of books have left me cold in the past. They have seemed almost unbelievable. I can't explain what it is about Oli's, but it's the exact opposite! I am so glad he has chosen to write this book!"
Jonathan Manning

"Oli's enthusiasm for life emanates through this book, and offers the reader an opportunity to consider different options for achieving a 'perfect lifestyle'. Oli offers some real, practical and helpful advice throughout his book."
Diane Toothill

"I find all the topics of many books are in Oli's "Table of contents". A great collection all in one place."
Maurice Chapman

"Oli is passionate about life. He is living the life that he is offering others in this book. Oli is handing you the keys to get maximum value."
Spencer Smith

"Great book! I like the style and content and the methodology outlined to the pathway to freedom."
Simon Laracy

"I have read your book and so did my boyfriend and we both found it not only interesting but also inspiring. There are a lot of things that you discuss that I have never known and now that I do I am going to make some big changes in my life especially where money is concerned."
Josephine O'Reilly

"I was impressed by the wide range of topics you covered contextually. Also, everything was put simply and most comprehensively."
Kees Bruin - Artist

"I found the book really interesting especially the first part and will be encouraging both my daughters 18 & 20 to read the book .It has also made me relook at my own life."
Yvonne Petheram

"I found the book very readable and engaging. I particularly enjoyed the practical and personal examples throughout the chapters which helped me make sense of the more technical/financial bits! The goal setting questionnaire at the beginning is a winner."
Sarah Hay

"Actually I was really surprised as I read different segments of this book just how captivated I was."
Brett Skjellerup

"I feel that the advice in this book has taught me foundational truths about my finances and simplified things about work and income that otherwise could have taken me ages to learn only through trial and error."
Ben Sainsbury

"Great book. It is so easy to read full of really practical and useful information. I've already learned a huge amount and plan to put it into practice."
Evan Williams

"I loved reading Oli Hille's book, it was addictive, I couldn't stop reading it, and would love to read the rest. It gave me heaps of ideas and really made me think about what I want out of life and the goals I need to set to be there. I now know I have the confidence to do whatever I set my mind to. Thanks Oli, Great Book."
Faye Summers

"I thought your book to be outstanding. I particularly got a lot out of the goal setting section. It is certainly a book I will use for continued reference. Why can't this sort of logic and style of thinking be taught at school?"
Brett Farmer

"I have just finished reading Creating the Perfect Lifestyle and thoroughly enjoyed it. I have read books from various authors such as Tony Robbins and Robert Kiyosaki and I would rate Oli Hille in the same class as these authors."
Simon Radtke

"This author has done an amazing job going through every aspect of our lives, inside and out, to give us a road map to our perfect life. This is not a guide to what you think a perfect life is, rather for what you want your life to be."
Veronika Tracy-Smith

"I could really identify with this book because I aspire to do the things that Oli does. This is a great peek into the businesses he uses to create financial freedom and the 'Perfect Lifestyle.' He exposes everything from how to get projects done on time to how to find your soul mate. Highly recommended!"
Hugh Kimura

"I recommend this book to anyone that is struggling with how to set their life on the right tracks."
Sherrie Giddens

"I am thrilled to have been introduced to this book. I find it exciting and so inspiring. It is highly readable and I am sure that the recipients of the copies I gave them for Christmas will benefit from reading it. Thank you Oli."
Jac

"I enjoyed this book and found it inspiring, concise, helpful and relevant. You definitely need a pad and pen whilst reading it, to plan out your goals, write out quotes to keep for inspiration and make notes for your own life. A very helpful book."
"The Kindle Book Review"

"I purchased this book a while ago, read and enjoyed it. Then I moved on. Yet I find myself returning to the practical wisdom of goal setting and then keeping a diary of those goals. There is actually much more than that I have learned from this practical guide so full of wisdom."
Alison Heath

"Honestly, I do no justice in reviewing this book. It's best you read it for yourself if you want a change in your circumstance and want to create the perfect lifestyle for yourself and family. Highly recommended."
Placida Acheru

"This is a great book, is a must read for teenagers. very well organized and informative, it inspired and motivated me a lot, we all deserve the lifestyle that we truly want, and this is the book that can guide you to the lifestyle that we want. Thank you Oli Hille for writing this wonderful piece."
Ronnie Sum

"I had already read some of Oli's other work but this book told a story... a story that captured the essence of everything you need to do to create your own perfect lifestyle. Thank you Oli for sharing this great book with us!"
Jane Kelly

"I read it beginning to end, and now I find myself returning to it as a guide for any area of life I feel needs work at that moment. I would suggest everyone get this book and use it as a daily reference to enhance your lifestyle. Thanks Oli for making it so simple to create the perfect lifestyle!"
Jeselle Eli

"Recently I had the pleasure of reading 'Creating the Perfect Lifestyle' and I can honestly say it's very inspiring and enjoyable to know what you can accomplish with your life if you just keep the proper mindset and attitude which Oli clearly demonstrates with his writing. A+++++++++++++"
Tim McManus

"My friend Oli Hille is "Living the Lifestyle" he talks about in the book."
Amid Yousef

"Over the last couple of years I've reflected on Oli's various written encouragements. They are words to the wise. I need reminding on keeping the main thing the main thing and Oli drives this principle home with power, along with a unique and believable presentation of immensely simple, practical and even more so achievable tactics."
Matt Harrington

"Great tips for those who are interested in changing their life style around and going for their passion."
Jeff Rivera

"One of the most empowering books I have read so far on Lifestyle and success. Oli Hille, is really a great writer. I kept on reading over and over again. A must read book."
Bernard Kelvin Clive

"I highly recommend it to those striving to become a better person enjoying one's unique daily life. The truth is we can never say we have arrived to the perfect lifestyle, which makes Oli's book even more valuable as a continual resource for daily meaningful living."
Delmy Vialpando

"Oli Hille's "Creating the Perfect Lifestyle" is a pitch-perfect compendium of the very best in self-help. Its friendly, practical approach to both inner and outer success makes it THE field-guide for a compelling future and, most importantly, an exceptional present."
Dino Palazzi

"There is much to learn from this book and if you take the advice seriously you could really improve your situation in life."
Rebecca Johnson, "The Rebecca Review", Amazon "Top 10" Reviewer

"Oli, I just finished your new book and I have the greatest feeling of Joy in my heart. My Father use to give advice to me, but it always felt like a General barking out orders. Reading Oli's book felt like sitting down with an old friend and sharing life stories and experiences. I enjoyed how you opened up and shared your stories of your success and failures along the way, but most of all the faith you have in the Lord. I love that you are brave enough to open up and share your faith with me. Faith in God, Love of Family and success a Perfect Lifestyle. Thank you!"
Terence Redmond

"There is a thread of positivity throughout the book that makes you want to keep on reading."
Ken Flugel

"I thoroughly enjoyed reading this book. However, what is more important, is I put some of the ideas and concepts into practise - and I even hit my own goal of writing a book after reading this . This book is about putting things into practise to change things – it's not a 'self help' book – it's a 'help yourself by doing' book!"
Richard Blakeborough

"I love how positive he is and in his book "Creating the Perfect Life Style" he fills the book with every possible area that can affect life, including health. This is more than just a book. It is a workbook. It is a life guide that can be referred to over and over again. Oli does not mind challenging traditional beliefs about how success is supposed to be. He encourages us to renew our minds and focus on the lifestyle we want. For anyone who is looking to improve their life, this book will quickly get you on the path to a quality life. This is a book that will become a part of my permanent library. I am glad I ran across it!"
Rhonda Clark

"Wish I had had a book like that when I was 18."
Andrew Buxton

"Oli's book makes the perfect life style closer than ever."
Marco Garito

"Very practical and easy to read!"
Ron Balzer

"Excellent, excellent book."
Clint Arthur

"Complete transformational, and informational journey to guide you to pastures new leaving no stone unturned, destined to help thousands and thousands around the world!"
Sally Francis

"I love "Creating the Perfect Lifestyle". I've been reading self help books for many years but this one makes the most sense to me. It's easy to read & never gets laborious. On my second reading of it now. Excellent."
Steve Mulry

Preface

The reason I wrote this book is that I wish I had this knowledge when I was just starting out. I want young people (of all ages) to have access to the secrets of successful living. I also want my three children to have a guide for when they start out on the biggest adventure of all – life!

Important

Life is not about getting everything you want all of the time. In this book the Perfect Lifestyle is not about always having everything go right for you. Rather it is about tackling the hurdles life puts in front of you and making the best possible life for yourself and those around you.

Disclaimer

Contents

Creating the Perfect Lifestyle

"It is God who arms me with strength and makes my way perfect." Psalm 18 v 32

Introduction

The purpose of this book is to help you decide on and then achieve your Perfect Lifestyle. By lifestyle I do not necessarily mean living the high life as a multi-millionaire. What I mean by lifestyle is your ideal way of living, and especially how you would like to live in five years time.

For you this might mean:

- Being debt free in a house you love, with a nice car and a vacation house by the sea;
- Owning your own scuba diving school;
- Working in your dream job;
- Being self-funded so you can spend all your time saving the environment;
- Being a missionary;
- Creating a boutique winery;
- Being able to give away $50,000 every year to people in need;
- Retiring at 45;
- Being a self-funded aid worker in the third world;
- Being an international entrepreneur with summer houses all over the world and your own private jet;
- Fighting poverty and injustice while your investments earn you passive income.

Whatever your definition of the Perfect Lifestyle, this book will help you achieve it.

According to research by Edgar Dale (1969) and his Cone of Learning, on average we only remember 10% of what we read. However we remember 90% of what we say and do.

To get the most out of this book:

- Do the exercises, make lots of notes; and
- Practice the techniques.

Perspective

This book is about creating your Perfect Lifestyle. However, the only reason we have the luxury of being able to plan a wonderful lifestyle is that we have our basic physical and psychological needs met. This is not the case for most people in the world. You may be familiar with the "State of the Village Report" which is a statistical analysis of the world's population as if the population was shrunk to 100 people. The original version was created by Donella Meadows.

Using this analysis, if the world's current population was 100, the world would look like this:

- 80 would live in substandard housing.
- 50 would be illiterate.
- 50 would suffer from malnutrition.
- 33 would not have access to clean, safe drinking water.
- 18 would live on less than US$1 per day.

The report states that if you have money in the bank, in your wallet, and spare change in a container somewhere, you are in the top 8% of the world's most wealthy people.

This book talks a lot about creating and retaining wealth. However we have to remember that in the big picture money itself is not all that important. Pursuing money and assets for their own sake is unwise because it ignores the fundamental aspects of creating a great lifestyle. Here is my list of the top ten things that are most important to me. You will notice that having money is not on this list:

1.   I experience peace, hope and love from my relationship with God.

2.   My children are healthy and happy.

3.   I have a happy marriage and family life.

4.   I am physically healthy.

5.   I am mentally healthy.

6.   I have good friends whom I love and who love me.

7.   I live in a peaceful and stable country.

8.   I have a stress free life.

9.   I have peace inside myself.

10.   I have a balanced lifestyle.

It is likely that right now or at times in your life you will not experience all of the top ten things that are most important to you. You might be physically unwell, you may have a sick child, high levels of stress, a business failure, or an unhappy family life. This does not mean you cannot achieve your Perfect Lifestyle. Life is not about getting everything you want all of the time. In this book, the Perfect Lifestyle is not about always having everything go right for you. Rather it is making the best possible life for yourself and those around you and successfully overcoming the obstacles life puts in front of you.

True Riches

Only you can decide your definition of wealth and lifestyle. I watched an adventure documentary recently, and one of the characters said that for him "true riches" was the opportunity to go in to the wild and climb cliffs and mountains. You probably already know or are on the path to knowing what "true riches" mean to you.

We all gravitate to those activities that really excite us. But too often we settle for something less, or end up watching on TV what we would love to be doing ourselves. As you read this book, make it clear in your mind that you are aiming for your Perfect Lifestyle, not a second hand version, not what your peers or parents or society expects.

You are in control of your life.

You define what "true riches" means to you.

YOU are about to create your Perfect Lifestyle.

Chapter 1 - Defining Your Perfect Lifestyle

Imagine the way you want your life to be in five years time:

- More Money?
- More Time?
- Excellent Health?
- More Fun?
- More Love?
- More Connection?
- Better Relationships?
- More Intimacy?
- Less Work?
- Less Stress?
- Less Uncertainty?
- More Passion?
- More Energy?
- More Creativity?
- More Freedom?
- More Joy?
- More Abundance?

Add your own desires to the list:

- _____

- _____

- _____

This book is all about taking you from where you are now to where you want to be.

Only you can decide what your Perfect Lifestyle will be, and only you can plan for it and make it happen. You need to realize that you can and will have the lifestyle you choose. Often we have been taught to react to what life throws at us rather than to be proactive and make life happen the way we want it to. Most of us have been socialized and educated to believe we cannot break out of what society and our peer group says is the norm.

For this reason when we read a statement like:

"I can have any lifestyle I choose."

- We don't believe it. If this is your reaction I recommend putting this statement in a prominent place on your wall or on a card by your bed and repeat it aloud two to three times a day.

This will re-program your mind to accept that you can achieve your Perfect Lifestyle. What usually holds us back the most is our own beliefs about what we can achieve. There literally is no limit to what your life can be. Anyone can plan to have a great lifestyle. I wish I had read a book like this when I was a teenager. But whatever your age, today is the day to start planning for a better life.

What lifestyle do you want?

Everyone is different, and no one can tell you what your Perfect Lifestyle can be. Sure, use your friends, your parents and your colleagues as a sounding board, but don't allow anyone to narrow your focus or undermine your dreams.

First, you have to dream. You probably already daydream about how you would like to live. If not, allow yourself to dream and dream big dreams. Having big dreams and big plans is crucial when you are getting ready to create your Perfect Lifestyle. If you plan for a mediocre and just-get-by lifestyle, that is what you will achieve. If you have a huge and passionate plan, you will almost certainly achieve a huge and passion-filled lifestyle. Don't follow the crowd or allow yourself to be squeezed into a mould that has been made for you by others' expectations.

Here are two quotes I love:

"If you never dream, you can never have a dream come true."
Anonymous

*"Your dreams **are** your real job."*
Joyce Spizer

A Note of Caution

Lives that achieve greatness always require sacrifice. Think about anyone who has made a huge positive impact on the world. Their life involved sacrifice.

Examples include:

Mother Teresa
Martin Luther King
Gandhi

A friend of mine sent me this recently:

Melanae grew up in Karlsruhe a beautiful city in southern Germany. It is located in one of the richest parts of southern Europe only a short drive from Switzerland. The city is full of quaint cafes and castles, and it is surrounded by beautiful vineyards and the

Black Forest. When I first met her she had a successful career and a great social life, but she was bored and lacked vision or purpose.

Now Melanae lives in "Crackland", a desperate urban hell in Sao Paulo, a vast city of 20 million people in Brazil. Crackland got its name from the many street children that live on its mean streets who are addicted to crack cocaine. One time when I was there, I saw a child that looked to be only 5 or 6 years old smoking crack curled up in a little ball on the filthy street.

Melanie now goes out with a team every week looking to rescue as many kids as she can. She shows God's love to these lost street kids, giving them medical attention, food and a safe place to sleep. When I saw Melanae after she had been working in Sao Paulo for almost two years, she was transformed. She has never looked more beautiful, so happy, so full of purpose and meaning. She has never been so alive because she has found her mission and her destiny.

Because the steps to creating a fantastic lifestyle are generic, you can use this book to create whatever lifestyle you choose. However if you choose to create a lifestyle that is built around getting more for yourself and not contributing, you risk missing out on what is most important: contentment, peace, abundance and love.

While you set about creating your Perfect Lifestyle, think about the ways you can use your talents and passions to make the world a better place. Remember that the people who achieve most usually make the biggest sacrifices.

"Great achievement is usually born of great sacrifice, and is never the result of selfishness."
Napoleon Hill

Dreaming Big

When it comes to planning your Perfect Lifestyle, it is too easy to fall into the trap of thinking small and dreaming small. This is a serious mistake. Remember you are about to plan the life of your dreams. This is not a time to be conservative or shy. This is the time to be imagining the best possible life for yourself and those around you.

Here are some examples of small dreams and big dreams:

Dreaming Small	**Dreaming Big**
To have a debt free house.	To have a beautiful, large debt free house with an acre of land and stables, right by the sea.
To travel business class.	To own my own jet.
To help the homeless in my neighbourhood.	To help the homeless in the whole country.
To own my own business.	To own my own business and earn $200,000 a year within four years and never work weekends.

To give $5,000 a year to charity.	To give $100,000 every year to charity.
To have happy healthy children.	To have happy healthy children who achieve great things and leave a positive mark on the world.
To have 80% of my present income when I retire.	To retire at 45 with passive income of over $500,000 per year.
To have a steady career.	To be the best person in my organization and to continually think about and suggest ways of improving what we do.
To be happy to wait until something better comes along.	To achieve my dreams by actively looking and trying new things.
To do the best I can in my job and support aid organizations with any excess cash.	To do whatever I can to make the world a better place and eradicate hunger and poverty in the poorest places in the world.

Questionnaire

One of the most important parts of this book is the following questionnaire. If you are serious about creating your Perfect Lifestyle, I recommend you complete this section. The questionnaire is only for your benefit. The answers will help you define your goals in order to perfect your lifestyle. And yes - please write in this book!

Questionnaire

1. What score out of 10 would you give your life today if a score of 10 means that you have achieved your perfect life?

———————

(If your score is 4 or below you need a radical lifestyle change.)

2. What would need to change in your life for you to be able to get a score of 10?

———————————————————————

———————————————————————

———————————————————————

3. What three things do you most want to achieve in the next year?

_____

_____

_____

4. What three things do you most want to achieve in your life?

_____

_____

_____

5. Imagine yourself at 85 years old looking back on your life. What sort of life would you like to be looking back on? Adventure? Success? Prosperity? Joy? Health?

_____

_____

_____

6. In ten years from now, what annual income would you like (remember to dream big)?

$_____

7. If you had a lot more time and a lot more money than you needed, what would you like to do to help others and make the world a better place?

_____

_____

_____

8. What steps could you take right now (TODAY) to take you towards what you have written down for points 3, 4, 5, 6, 7 (New job? More education? Making investments? Learning a language? Setting goals?)

_____

_____

_____

_____

Action Step 1:

Read back over your answers and make notes in the space below on thoughts that have come to mind while you completed the questionnaire. If it has been a long time since you thought about the direction of your life, these thoughts and ideas will be invaluable in the weeks to come.

Chapter 2 - My Lifestyle

Soon after I turned 30, I woke up one morning and I had a revelation:

Life is not about working your butt off for someone else, getting stressed, getting anxious, and squeezing what you really want to do into the little time you have left at the end of the day. No! **Life is actually about LIFESTYLE.**

In the last few years I have successfully set goals, made plans and achieved a fantastic lifestyle. It is a lifestyle that is right for me. I am not suggesting that my lifestyle is right for you. But one thing I am sure of - you can achieve the lifestyle of **your** dreams.

I am not telling you about my lifestyle to impress you, but rather to impress upon you that **you** can plan and design the lifestyle you want, and **you** can set goals and achieve your Perfect Lifestyle.

I live in the country I most want to live in – New Zealand. I live in the suburb I most want to live in. I have a relationship with God that gives my life meaning and a purpose. I have a happy marriage and three beautiful children. I live in a lovely big house 150 yards (meters) from the sea. While our children were at pre-school my wife chose to be a full time Mom, and the fact that we could afford to do this took a lot of stress away from our family.

For the last few years I have worked around 20 hours a week (this does not include writing, research, charity work, and reading). I love the work I do, and I look forward to going to my office. Now that all of my children are at school, I have moved my office home. My office is modern, spacious and comfortable. I work around my family's needs which come first. I have breakfast with my kids, and I see them off to school.

I earn money in five ways that perfectly suit the way I want to live:

- Semi-passive rental income from real estate;
- Semi-passive income from internet based business;
- Passive income from investments;
- Trading the financial markets;
- Lecturing and mentoring;
- Writing.

One of the advantages of having different income streams is that you have some protection if you have a bad year in one of your ventures. No venture is wildly successful every year, and in some ventures, in some years you lose money. I recommend you start to think about how you can have multiple income streams.

Because of the way I work, I have a lot of time in my "business week". I use this time to do a lot of things I enjoy:

1. Exercise.
2. Prayer.
3. Spending time with friends.
4. Meeting new people.
5. Writing.
6. Reading.
7. Exploring new business opportunities.
8. Taking additional time for my family.

I also spend time every week doing work for two charities, one international and one local. I also teach Bible in Schools for an hour a week at a local school. I regularly mentor people.

I take time out of my "business week" for my family. In the last five years, I have missed only two of my children's sporting or cultural events (out of dozens). Both times I was overseas. I take days off to take my kids fishing. I take mornings off to be "Dad helper" with my kids school activities. I go to school assemblies to video my kids if they are performing or getting a prize.

From 1999 to 2009 I took nine weeks vacation with my family every year. In 2005 and again in 2009, I took two full months off for family vacations in Europe.

I estimate I feel stressed perhaps three or four days a year.

There are very few things in my life I don't look forward to. Each new day brings interest, fun, fulfillment, challenge and enjoyment.

We have enough disposable income to provide for our needs, have some of our "wants" and to give money to people in need.

I'm not interested in making lots of money as such (except I have big goals in relation to the amount I want to give away). What I am really interested in is creating a lifestyle that gives me the time and energy to give to the most important things in my life:

1. Following Jesus.
2. Building the Kingdom of God.
3. Spending time with my family.
4. Spending time with my friends.
5. Keeping fit and healthy.
6. Being creative.

Your list of what is most important to you may be quite different. But whatever is on your list you will only be content and fulfilled if you develop a lifestyle that allows you to concentrate on those things rather than trying to squeeze them in to an already overly busy, financially stretched, and stressed life.

I have deliberately chosen businesses that fit into the lifestyle I want to live. My businesses are internet and email based. This means I can run them from anywhere I can get internet access, i.e. anywhere in the world. Any phone calls can be diverted to my mobile phone or any other land-line, so I don't have to be in my office at any particular time of the day. As I said, I love what I do so none of it feels like work.

I deliberately do not have a Blackberry or PDA, and I do not receive emails on my mobile phone. There are plenty of new gadgets that allow you to work or keep in touch with work 24/7, but why? My advice is just say no to anything that allows you or requires you to work when you don't need to or on weekends or vacations. Life is for living and learning and family and friends and spirituality and bettering yourself – not being a slave to your business or your boss.

Chapter 3 - Goals

Setting goals is the single most important step you will make in creating your Perfect Lifestyle. Spending **one hour today** setting and writing out your goals will give you the biggest return for an hour's work you will ever receive.

Critical Principle 1: **The best return on your time (ever) will be the time you spend setting goals.**

Every successful person, successful business and successful sports team sets goals. You **cannot** achieve your Perfect Lifestyle unless you set goals and put strategies in place to achieve those goals.

Each goal must have three attributes:

1. It must be achievable.
2. It cannot be too easy to achieve.
3. It must be measurable.

The following statement for example is not a goal:

To earn a higher income.

Whereas the following statement is a goal:

To increase my income by 30% by the end of next year.

First, it is achievable, second it will require you to make some changes in order to achieve it and third, on 31 December next year, you will know exactly whether you achieved your goal or not.

Add Power to Your Goal Setting

There are three critical techniques to make your goals more powerful:

1. Write them down.
2. Review them regularly.
3. Commit key goals to accountability partners.

It is important to remember that dreams are not goals. Your dream might be to climb to the top of the seven highest mountains in the world. You can day-dream about it and talk about and read about it until you are too old to actually do it. But, if you make a goal that you are going to climb these peaks within three years, then suddenly you have to start planning and saving and preparing. If you put this goal on your wall, make it a priority, and tell your friends and family, you will achieve your goal.

There is a perfect time to set your goals – **Right Now**!

I suggest you stop reading, get a pen and complete the following goal setting exercise.

Goal Setting Exercise

This is a vitally important exercise that literally has the power to transform your life in a very short period of time.

You need to set a number (at least ten) of specific goals for your life. Make these goals ones that if you achieve them will radically improve your life and Lifestyle.

Remember you must make each goal achievable, measurable, and a stretch.

You may want to set goals for a number of different timeframes i.e. Daily, Weekly, Annual and Long Term.

Part 1 – Set Your Initial Goals

Set at least one goal for each of the following:

- Income;
- Health/Exercise;
- Relationships;
- Career;
- Personal Interests (for example travel, hobbies);
- Creative;
- Spiritual;
- Investment;
- Educational;
- Contributing/Giving.

Complete the list on the next page.

Specific Goal	Achieve by date
1.	
2.	
3.	
4.	
5.	
6.	
7.	
8.	
9.	
10.	
11.	
12.	
13.	
14.	

This is not your finalized goals list but it is a good start. It is important you do not overload yourself with goals. Ideally, your personal goals should fit easily onto a standard sized piece of paper. You should be able to review it quickly to see where you are at.

Part 2 - Think Through Your Goals

It is worthwhile thinking over your goals, especially if this is the first time you have ever done it. Take a couple of days to think about where you ideally want to be in five years (and longer) and what goals you need to set in order to get there. In a day or two, re-work your goals so you are happy with them, and then transfer them to a standard sized piece of paper. Then laminate the sheet and put it up in your shower so you can review your goals every day.

Your goals need to be regularly updated as you and your lifestyle changes. You may need to re-write some of your goals every few weeks. This is an important part of the process and it is fun.

When you have finished your goals list, it will look something like this example:

Daily Goals

1. Eat five servings of fresh fruit and vegetables.
2. Get up at 6am and go for a walk or exercise.
3. Read one chapter of a book.

Weekly Goals

1. Exercise three times a week.
2. Read one book per week.
3. Spend an hour one-on-one with each of my children.
4. Spend four hours practising guitar.

In the Next Year Goals

1. To lose five pounds (three kilograms) by 31 December.
2. To purchase a rental property by 30 November.
3. To join a rock band by 30 June.
4. To read three motivational books and go to one motivational seminar by 31 October.
5. To start sponsoring a child in the developing world within three months.
6. To increase my income by 20% in the next year.

Long Term Goals

1. To be debt free within ten years.
2. To run a marathon within three years.
3. To be able to retire at 50 with a passive income of $150,000 a year.
4. To be able to spend 10 hours a week working with people in need within five years.
5. To have a business earning a net income of $100,000 within five years.

Part 3 – Create Your Standard Sized Goals List

Now you need to prioritize your goals and print them on to one standard size sheet of paper. Use the guide above and break your goals into:

Daily
Weekly
12 Months
Long Term

Part 4 - Pick Your Three Most Important Goals

Go through your goals list and pick the three most important goals. These are the ones that if you achieve them will have the greatest positive impact on your life.

Choose two people you really respect and email them telling them that you are committing to them that you will achieve the goals. Ask them to keep you on track, and tell them you will update them in one month. These are your accountability partners.

Part 5 - Review Your Goals Weekly

At least once a week review your goals list. Modify and change where necessary. Remember your goals list is a living, breathing creature. It is not an engraved block of stone!

Part 6 - One Month Review

Set a reminder in your phone or your calendar to completely review your goals one month after you first set them.

Have you set goals that are too easy?
Have you set goals that are too difficult?
Have you achieved some "one year" goals already?
Have your circumstances changed?

Rewrite your goals list at this point. Once again print them on a standard size piece of paper.

You now need to email your two accountability partners and update them on how you are progressing with your three goals.

Summary

If you diligently follow this simple eight part process, no-one and nothing will get in the way of you achieving your goals.

Clear everything else off your calendar and complete this process.

Do it now!

Tick Lists

You may also need to have a separate page as a tick-list. For example, on my wall in my office, I have my goal's list (and one in my shower). Next to it I have a sheet I fill in for my exercise goals. My exercise goal is to complete 150 exercise sessions a year – either in the gym, on my bike or swimming. On the check sheet I have 150 squares. I tick one each time I complete an exercise session. This way I know exactly where I am at with my goal. If I do less than three sessions in a week I know I am falling behind my schedule.

Lifetime Goals

There are a separate set of goals I call Lifetime Goals. Since the movie "The Bucket List", some people say "That goal is going on my bucket list" i.e. they aim to achieve the goal before they kick the bucket!

It is great to have Lifetime Goals. They don't have a specific achievement date but clearly they have a finite time period - before you die. Of course the goal may also be constrained by your age and health. You may not be able to climb Mount Everest at 90 years old.

I encourage you to write a list of 100 Lifetime Goals. Make them so wonderful that it will be a momentous day in your life when you achieve them. Make the goals fun, some easy to achieve some very difficult. Some will be goals you may only get one or two chances in your lifetime to achieve. One of my Lifetime Goals is to walk on the moon. I've had this goal since the early 1980s. Back then people just thought I was crazy. Now that commercial flights into space are in the planning stage people still laugh at my goal, but now they're not so sure!

I am sure you have some Lifetime Goals, but you may never have put pen to paper. Remember writing down goals makes them more powerful. Reviewing them regularly forces your mind to think about how and when you can achieve you goal.

For example, say one of your life time goals is to visit the Great Wall of China. If you are reviewing your goals regularly, you might remember you have a conference in Hong Kong and have a spare day in your schedule. It is an easy flight from Hong Kong. If you hadn't written it down and reviewed this goal, you may have just had a shopping day in Hong Kong instead.

Other Goals

You might have some other specific goals you want to make a list for. I know people (myself included) who have a list of people they would like to meet. Once again if you write down goals and review them regularly, life has the habit of hugely increasing the probability of those goals being achieved.

Whatever dreams, aspirations and wants you have, make them into a goals list. Write them down and review them regularly. You will be amazed how effective this simple strategy is.

Brian Tracy's Goal Strategy

I have started using a strategy of Brian Tracy's which I have found to be useful.

"Rewrite your major goals every day, in the present tense, exactly as if they already existed."
Brian Tracy

This is effective for a number of reasons. First it focuses you on your major goals every day. Second it puts you in the positive frame of mind because you feel like you have already achieved your goals. And third it activates the law of attraction to bring your goals to reality.

Try it! I have found it to be very powerful.

Chapter 4 - To Do Lists

One of the most effective time planning tools is the "To Do" list. If you have a continually updated list of things you need to achieve and their respective priorities, it is far easier to be focused and manage your time wisely. All successful people use To Do lists.

I have three types of To Do lists. The main one is a general list of things I have to do in the next week or two. It is split into the top half which is work related and the bottom half which is personal.

The second list is a daily "Must Do" list which will typically have that day's priorities plus appointments. In general this list will not have more than 10 items as it is better to complete the list than run out of time.

I have recently expanded this list so that either on a Sunday night or Monday morning, I will rule up one piece of standard size paper with five separate sections for:

Monday
Tuesday
Wednesday
Thursday
Friday

Under each day I will write out the most important five to seven tasks I want to accomplish. While I could just as easily do this on a calendar or print out my Outlook calendar, there is something about writing it all out that focuses my mind on planning each day of the coming week. It is also easy to carry forward any tasks that didn't get done on one day, to the next. Also doing it on a Sunday night forces your mind to start planning ahead. This is an excellent strategy to improve your efficiency and time management.

The third list is a "To Do in Town" list. I live 10 miles (15km) from the city, so I minimize my trips into town by only going in once a week or once a fortnight. Every time I think of something I need in town I put it on this list. Whenever I go to town I have seven or eight things to do, and I can race around, do them all and not waste any time.

It doesn't matter where you keep your list – your computer, PDA, mobile phone or on paper. Paper works best for me.

Another advantage of To Do lists is you never miss an appointment or a deadline. I often highlight appointments so that I make sure I don't miss one. I also use the reminder function on my mobile phone as a back-up.

If you have trouble managing your daily tasks or your time, start using To Do lists.

Chapter 5 - Gifts and Abilities Part 1

In life you have two or three things you are really good at. I am going to refer to these as your gifts and abilities.

It is possible, perhaps even probable that you have not completely discovered or developed these gifts and abilities. In my life for example, I find myself slowly gravitating towards what I am best at. Some people know very early in life what their real gifts are but for many of us it takes time.

Remember when you were in school? Your favorite subject was always the one you were best at. It came naturally, and it always felt good to succeed easily. You looked forward to that class, and you were happy whilst doing it. I expect you could quickly pick from this list the subjects you most enjoyed:

- English
- Mathematics
- Science
- Geography
- History
- Art
- Sport
- Music

Of course these are just school subjects, and this list represents only a tiny fraction of the potential interests and possibilities in life.

However, the principle is the same. The activities you are best at you enjoy. Doing them brings more feelings of achievement, happiness and excitement.

This is one of the best ways to find your true gifts and abilities. Continue to gravitate towards the things that interest and excite you. If you are dissatisfied with your life or your career, it is because you have fallen into or accepted a way of life or a job that is not aligned to your gifts and abilities. If that is you, make a change NOW. If you don't, you will sit in your rocking chair at 85, looking back in regret.

We can only find true happiness and an abundant life when we are in that place. That is why it is so disappointing to see people who:

a) Forget what really excites them and fall into a job that wears them down year after year.

b) Lack energy and motivation to make real change happen in their lives.

c) Waste time (for example TV and trashy novels) rather than doing what they were called to do.

d) Misuse their gifts and abilities and make the world a worse place (for example Hitler and Bernie Madoff).

e) Give up when they need to push through the many barriers life puts in their way.

Most people have just two or three gifts or abilities. It is important to identify what these are and then pursue them with all of your energy. It is frustrating and counter-productive to try and be something you were not created to be. Sure with hard work and determination you can be above average at just about anything. But you are selling yourself short if you are striving to be outstanding in an area outside of your God given gifts and abilities.

The first challenge for many people is they don't know what their true gifts are. My advice is to always gravitate towards what you love and what your heart leads you to. Attend seminars, do courses and read books that are designed to help you to find your true gift. Also, ask friends who you trust what they see as your gifts and abilities.

The second challenge for many people, when they do find their true gift, is seeing a way to make it a career or vocation. In most cases it is easier and more financially rewarding to follow a traditional career path. Consider someone whose gift is to advocate for the poor and disenfranchised. There is no easy and lucrative career path for him/her. It is far easier to put that gift aside and take a corporate job with a defined career path. But although it is easier and more financially rewarding, that person will never be fulfilled or satisfied in that corporate job. I loved the fantastic saxophonist Michael Brecker whose family wanted and expected him to be a doctor. But he followed his dream and his gift and became a sensational musician.

Life is not about taking the easy option and the "easiest" financial gain. Imagine if Claude Monet, Mother Teresa, Charles Dickens and Shakespeare had taken the easy and financially secure option.

I like what Malcolm Forbes the publisher of Forbes Magazine said in these two quotes:

"The biggest mistake people make in life is not trying to make a living at doing what they most enjoy."

"Success follows from what you want to do. There is no other way to be successful."

I also like what Jack Canfield said in his book "The Success Principles":

"You were born with an inner guidance system that tells you when you are on or off purpose by the amount of joy you are experiencing. The things that bring you the greatest joy are in alignment with your purpose."

You need to do your part. Forget the easy option. Forget settling for a comfortable income. Find your gift, live your dream and change the world!

There are only two reasons why people do not live an abundant life:

a) They are on the wrong path and have settled for a lower calling; or

b) They are on the journey towards the life they were called to live, and they are experiencing the normal challenges and obstacles that everyone faces.

But remember, an abundant life does not equal an easy life without challenges and difficulties. Look at Mother Teresa's life. It was tremendously abundant, but it was not easy or simple or prosperous. But would she have exchanged her life for living in wealth and ease? Never! It was not what she was created for and called to.

Chapter 6 - Your Career

Remember the career advice you received at school? You fill out a form or a computer program on your likes and dislikes and aptitudes. It spits out a list of traditional dead-end, zero-fun, mind-numbing jobs. The list never includes dream-fulfilling opportunities: guitar hero, treasure hunter, explorer, urban artist, astronaut, trader or author.

Even more important it ignores the far more important life choices such as:

- Work just a few hours a week and spend the rest of the time (insert your ideal activity here) – for example saving the planet, reading every science fiction book ever written, building the kingdom of God, surfing, traveling the world.
- Find my true vocation where I love it so much it isn't work, it's joy.
- I don't know what I want to do and I don't care. I'm going to start doing the things I love doing and never compromise. I am going to keep gravitating to what I love until I find my place in the world.

All careers' advisor jobs should be terminated. The world would be a far better place if all careers advice offices had no people, just a sign that said "Take form".

The form would say this:

- Do what you love doing.
- Don't compromise.
- Ignore your income.
- Become the best you can be.
- Change the world.

"Look for a situation in which your work will give you as much happiness as your spare time."
Pablo Picasso

"You know you are on the road to success if you would do your job, and not be paid for it."
Oprah Winfrey

Chapter 7 - Income Choices: Employment

There are three main ways in which people earn income:

1. Employment
2. Owning a Business
3. Real Estate

The first two will be discussed in the following two chapters.

Of these three, the most limiting, and the least flexible and with the least chance of creating a lifestyle is employment.

"Employee of the month is a good example of how somebody can be both a winner and a loser at the same time."
Demetri Martin

You work for someone else and your income is limited by the hours you work, and in some cases, by the commissions you earn. If you take a year off, you receive nothing. Strangely "finding a job" is what we are told to do by our parents, our schools, our Technical Institutes and our Universities. We have not been taught to be entrepreneurs, business owners, real estate owners or developers. This is partly because the economy needs employees so businesses and state-owned enterprises can succeed. But most of the time being employed is not the road to your Perfect Lifestyle.

This is not to say that for some people being employed is exceptionally beneficial. For example my wife Fleur is a nurse. There is no job she loves more than helping and nursing sick people. For her, working as a nurse is part of her Perfect Lifestyle. She is not interested in turning this passion into a business. She is not interested in owning a private hospital or a nursing employment agency. What she loves is actually being with patients and nursing them. You may be the same. What you really enjoy in a job may primarily only exist in an employee role. Once again it is about identifying your passions and what you really enjoy. If being an employee is what you really love, I encourage you to stay employed.

At the same time, I would also encourage you to find ways to turn your passion into a separate income source or to develop a secondary income source. Even if being employed is something you love, your ideal lifestyle might mean only working four days a week, or never doing overtime, or having seven weeks annual vacation a year. Think about ways you can achieve these goals too. Remember you can often turn your work passion (in fact any passion) into a successful business. If you are being employed or you are training for employment, look for ways to start a business in that area.

I understand that business and real estate are not for everyone. They may not even be for most people. But if you want to create a fantastic lifestyle, it is unlikely you will succeed if you are only an employee. Fleur would be the first to agree that we wouldn't have anywhere near our current lifestyle if we lived on her nursing salary, even if it was combined with a salary I could earn as an employee.

Working for someone else is not usually the road to freedom (and wealth if that is what you are interested in). However, it can be useful when you start out. But if you do start out working for someone else, remember these golden rules:

1. Search for a job that involves something you love or are passionate about. Try to ensure you will be working with great people who will challenge and stimulate you to grow.

2. Your job is a stepping stone, not a destination.

3. Be willing to change your employer regularly, every 18 months or so. This enables you to gravitate more and more towards your passion. It also forces you to grow and learn at a faster pace.

4. Always be on the lookout for opportunities and people who will help you move towards your life of freedom and your perfect career.

5. Learn as much as you can from everyone you can (including customers and suppliers and top management). In the 21st Century people who can understand and manage the multiple functions of an organization will be very well rewarded - especially when it is your own organization.

6. Do not be influenced by the income. As long as you can afford to live, it should not come in to the equation.

Chapter 8 - Income Choices: Own Business

One of the best ways to create your Perfect Lifestyle is to start your own business. If you get it right, your own business can give you:

- A much higher income than employment.
- The ability to do something you love and are passionate about.
- A lifestyle that allows you to earn business income even when you are not working.
- The opportunity to choose when and where you work.
- The opportunity to structure your work around family.

By now you should be excited about starting your own business. Here are some key tips:

1. You are Unlikely to Make Profits Straight Away

Building a business takes time, patience and at least a little money. It is never a cash-tap. You cannot start a business and expect a week later to turn on a tap and have cash flowing out faster than you can count it. In fact, in the first year you might put more cash in than you take out.

2. Start While you are Employed (or Studying)

One of the great things about starting a business is that you can start small and grow bigger. If you are employed (or studying), start your business now and manage it in your spare time. As it grows and becomes profitable, you can reduce your employment or resign altogether.

When I first started my recruitment business, I worked two days as an accountant. This enabled me to keep going even though the business didn't make a profit for over a year.

3. Do a Budget

It is so tempting to avoid this step because by nature people who start their own businesses are optimistic about its success. However, you must do a budget and be conservative.

You must know your average weekly expenses. You must know the amount of income you make on each sale (margin). You must know your break-even sales level (i.e. how many goods and services you need to sell to cover your expenses).

Your budget only needs to be a simple spreadsheet with the money you have available (capital), any money you have borrowed, all business expenses (including start-up expenses like a computer) and any income you are making or expect to make.

You need to budget a year in advance, and you may need to update your budget every month. Your budget will tell you where the financial strengths and weaknesses are in your business. More critically, it will tell you what you need to achieve in order to make a profit.

It is vitally important not to over-estimate your income. Let's say your business is importing a new toy into the country, and you plan to sell it online. It is naïve to say: "There are 500,000 children in my target age bracket and 1 in 10 will buy my toy for Christmas, therefore I will sell 50,000 toys." It is far wiser to say "I will try to sell

500 toys, if I sell out, great I will order more." You also should ask your friends and family their opinion. They will help you to be realistic.

4. Avoid Retail Shops

I know that people make money in retail shops but I don't recommend it. Here is why:

(a) Long hours: you become a slave to your opening hours, including late nights and weekends. You have to be open otherwise your customers will not come back. You can't take time off easily, and you have to rely on staff.

(b) Staff: most small business owners will tell you the biggest headache is staff. Finding them, motivating them, training them, keeping them, and firing them! Try to avoid a reliance on a lot of staff especially while you are managing it all.

(c) Your lease: you are also a slave to your lease and your premises. If business is slow, the lease still has to be paid.

Remember the point of owning a business is to give you a lifestyle not more commitments. Starting your own café sounds romantic and easy. Ask a café owner – it isn't!

Of course if you want to be a retailer, there is a fantastic way to do it – via the Internet.

See point 14 for more on this.

5. Set up Good Systems

From day one of your new business get your systems in place. For example:

- Technology
- Accounting and tax
- Database of customers
- Ordering
- Stock control
- Invoicing
- Banking

At the beginning is the time to get this right and learn about the things you don't know. Once your business starts growing you won't have time to go back and get this right. When times are busy you will need your valuable time to grow and manage the business.

6. Run With Your Passions

One of the most exciting things about starting your own business is that you can let it grow out of your passions, interests and hobbies. As I said earlier, when you were at school you enjoyed the subjects you were best at. It was more enjoyable to spend time on the subjects you liked and were good at. The same is true of work and business. You will enjoy going to work and building your business if you start a business in an area you already like.

Action Step 2:

On a blank piece of paper write a list of everything you are passionate about, every interest, and every hobby. Don't think about business ideas, just write things down.

Now go through your list and think what possible business application there are. Here are some examples:

Interests	Possible Business Applications
Tea	Tea leaf import and online sales.
Sport	Online memorabilia auctions.
Astronomy	Subscription newsletter or web based home study program.
Cars	Online sales.
Golf	Parallel import of golf balls.
Farming	Arrange international experts to speak at conferences.
Movies	Make your own advertisements for popular products and try to sell them to the manufacturers as advertising on YouTube.

7. Leverage Your Knowledge

Statistics tell us that most people start their own business in an area they have already worked, or an area they have knowledge of. This makes a lot of sense. You are more likely to be successful if you start a business in an industry you know. You can probably spot a niche in your current market.

Example: Say you are a travel agent and your agency gets calls or emails every week from overseas people wanting a pre-organized motorbike trip of a particular location. Because there is nothing available, your agency has to turn them all down. While still working you set up a guided motorbike business, and on the day you resign you tell your boss about your new business and you offer their agency a generous cut of any business they send your way.

No matter what your interests are, there will be a business application. If you can't think of any, go to Google and type in your particular interest or business and see what comes up!

8. Business Has to be Fun

One of the most motivating aspects of owning your own business is that it is fun. Successful business owners nearly always have a good time doing business.

If you are not having fun in your job or your business it is time you had a lifestyle change.

Life is too short to have a work week that is not enjoyable. How much you enjoy your work impacts the rest of your life. But if you own a business that follows your passions and interests, you are most of the way towards enjoying your work life.

The phrase "fun rut" is an oxymoron, it is mutually exclusive. You just can't have fun if you're in a rut, and if you have been doing the same old thing for years. In business you have to keep doing new and different things, and that is half the fun.

Here are some examples of having fun in business:

- Meeting people with similar interests and passions to you.
- Writing your own advertisements.

- Checking your emails to see how many new orders you have.
- Answering the phone and taking the "money call". For example a huge order.
- Checking products you are selling on an auction site to see how many bids there are at what price.
- Diverting your phone to your mobile phone and going to your favorite café with a friend. My motto is that if I have my mobile phone with me, I'm working. This includes going to the gym too!
- Making big and exciting plans for your business.

For me, the most fun and rewarding part of owning a business is putting a successful deal together. It is a great feeling to think up a plan, put it together, have it work and make a nice profit at the end. I get a feeling of satisfaction that is far better than when I was a small part of a corporate success as an employee.

You must start your business with a sense of excitement and fun. If you don't have that – find a different business.

9. Surround Yourself with Positive People

This is a principle that applies to every aspect of life, but it is critical in business. Make sure you associate with people who are positive, encouraging and optimistic. You need a lot of energy and enthusiasm in business, especially when business is slow or when things go wrong. If you are surrounded by positive people, your energy will stay positive. But if you listen to pessimists and nay-sayers and people with no imagination, it will be difficult to get out of bed, let alone run a successful business!

10. Choose a Business Partner Carefully

I don't recommend a business partner if you are starting a new business, but if you have to have one, choose carefully. A business partnership is much like a marriage. Both partners have to have the same aims and goals. Only choose a business partner who is positive, hard working and fun to work with.

11. Having Shareholders

In some cases you may need to finance your business to a much higher level than you can afford. In this case, it is an option to have shareholders (investors) put money into your business. This can be an excellent way to raise capital for your business. However you need to be aware that once you have shareholders you are likely to have to submit your plans and ideas to them before you act. This does two things; it slows down your decision making, and it can mean having to run big decisions past your shareholders for approval. If it is just your business you can make your own decisions. Sometimes in business you need to move fast.

Here are two examples of highly successful people who do not have shareholders:

Richard Branson – Hugely successful without shareholders. Took his airline company Virgin Atlantic public (i.e. lots of shareholders) and regretted it. He ended up buying the shares back.

Donald Trump – Hugely successful without shareholders.

My point is, you can be very effective and successful without taking on shareholders. Of course having shareholders can mean huge success if you have the right sort of product. Bill Gates (Microsoft), Michael Dell (Dell Computers) and Steve Jobs (Apple computers) are obvious examples and all are billionaires.

12. Long Term Planning and Exit Strategy

Remember life is about lifestyle. You are not just starting a business for fun and excitement. You need to have a long-term plan for your business. Your long term plan must involve giving you the lifestyle you planned out in Chapter One.

I can't tell you exactly what your plan is because not everyone's lifestyle goal is the same. However, it should include the following:

Financial Freedom

At some time in the future you need to have the financial freedom to do some things you really want to do for example aid work in the third world, a summer in Italy, voluntary work at a local mission, be a travelling fan with a sports team - whatever!

Time

One of the long term goals of your business should be to free up more of your valuable time:

- Time for your family.
- Time for your friends.
- Time for your partner.
- Time for yourself.
- Time for exercise.
- Time for spirituality.

The key to happiness is working four to six hours a day according to a recent report. Dr Caroline West of Sydney University reported that while work delivers self-esteem, income and social ties, more than four to six hours a day will bring anxiety, exhaustion and a poor quality of life.

"We've structured our lives so the majority of our waking life is devoted to work, which might bring us more money but doesn't make us more fulfilled," Dr West said.

"So long as there's a trend to work these really long hours you'll continue to see the plateauing and decline of people's wellbeing."

Self Esteem

Your business should enhance the feeling that you are doing something useful, successful and something you are proud of.

You also need to think about your "exit strategy". This means, what is going to happen to my business in the long run? Some possibilities are:

- Pay a manager to run it for you and live off the residual income.
- Sell it to a competitor.
- Sell the business to new owner.
- Let the business wind down and you retire.
- Franchise it.
- Leave it to your children.
- Make it a public company by listing it on the stock market.
- Keep running it into your retirement.

13. Don't Just Own a Job

A final warning – there is a huge difference between owning a job and owning a business. A dentist who goes into private practise owns a job not a business. His/her income is based solely on the hours worked and/or patients seen. Similarly, if you buy a retail shop, you own a job that requires you to work huge hours.

You only really own a business when:

- It allows you to live a wonderful lifestyle; and
- It still keeps making profits regardless of whether you are working or not.

Sometimes it's even better to be employed than to "own a job". When you own a job you have long hours and you are responsible for the success of the business.

The exception to this rule is if you have a definite and written down plan to have employees take over the work you are doing, then for a short period you can own the job before passing it on to others and managing the business and keeping the profits.

You should now be excited and ready to start planning a new business. If you have some ideas going around in your head now, stop reading! Grab a blank piece of paper and start planning what you are going to do and how you are going to do it!

14. Two Ebooks

If you are interested in starting your own business, or you want to understand the Internet and Social Media better, I have written two comprehensive Ebooks based on my years of online business and the tens of thousands of dollars I have spent on courses, education etc.

Book 1: Internet Marketing for Business, Lifestyle, Influence and Income.

$2.99 from Amazon:

www.Amazon.com/dp/B006QRICEM

Book 2: Social Media for Business, Lifestyle, Influence and Income.

$2.99 from Amazon:

www.Amazon.com/dp/B006OU7UFS

These books will be an invaluable resource. I recommend you purchase them now.

Chapter 9 - The Best Game in the World

I am including this chapter for two reasons. First, because a lot of people first heard about me through the media coverage of this "game", and second because it is one of the five ways in which I earn the money that has enabled me to live a wonderful lifestyle.

I have experienced a large number of employment and business situations. I have read accounts of dozens of others. Of all of these there is one and only one that is pure. By pure I mean at the end of the day there is no doubt about the result of your efforts. In fact the result stares at you in black and white.

There are no employers to tell you how to do it. There are no employees to train and supervise.

There are no overheads. There are no excuses. There is just you, your decision making and the result.

There is no advertising, no answering the phone, no customers, no inventory, no database, no marketing, no cold-calling, no bad debts, no set hours, no set schedule. Just you, your decisions and the result.

Even better, you are playing a giant game with players all over the world. When you get good enough to win regularly you get paid – a lot!

And it gets even better. The game is so vast and covers so many possibilities you can choose which sub-game you want to play. So you can choose a part of it that fits with your personality, with your strengths, with your sleep patterns, with your timeframes and your thresholds, using strategies that suit you. While there are some basic rules of play, you can develop entirely your own personal rules to win the game!

It's the purest game of all and you can make a living or a fortune playing it.

What is the name of this game?

Trading!

I have been trading foreign currencies and commodities part time since 1990. Let me tell you how I first started.

In 1990 when I was 25 I received an inheritance of $30,000. That was back when $30,000 was a lot of money! I must have been reading a lot of James Bond novels at the time because I thought it would be really cool to open a Swiss bank account. I applied to Credit Suisse for the account forms and while I waited for them to arrive, I decided to put my dollars into Swiss Francs.

At that time there was one dealing room in the city I lived in. I phoned them up and did the deal – I still remember the rate 0.8334! So my $30,000 became 25,002 Swiss Francs.

Three weeks later the bank documents arrived from Switzerland. I phoned the bank to talk about transferring the money. The broker told me the exchange rate had moved in my favor. I asked him what he meant. He said the exchange rate was now 0.7962 and that if transferred the Swiss Francs back into dollars I would have $31,400. I said "Do it! Do it now!"

When I put the phone down I jumped around the house whooping with delight. I couldn't believe I had just made $1,400 for doing nothing.

The vacation job I had just finished paid $8.60 an hour which was $275 a week after tax. I had just made the equivalent of five weeks of early starts and hard dirty work – just by making two phone calls! I changed my mind about opening a Swiss bank account and instead I started to move my money in and out of currencies. In retrospect it was a very inefficient way to trade currencies but at the time I didn't know any better. Surprisingly I did six profitable trades in a row and made a few thousand dollars – I literally could not believe it!

Back in 1990 there was no internet, and it was very difficult to check prices and movements unless you phoned your broker. However, I was studying at university and Reuters had sponsored a live trading screen at the library. I could check my profits and losses between classes! I had a friend at university who had some money so we started trading together.

As I learned more I started trading metals and commodities such as gold and cocoa. I was flying by the seat of my pants, and I had no real idea what I was doing. Consequently I had some significant losses followed by that awful feeling in the pit of your stomach.

Like anything, the more you do it the better and smarter you become. I have made *lots* of mistakes in trading but most of these have been real learning opportunities. Losing hard-earned cash is a good way to learn fast. You never want to make the same mistake twice.

I want to make it clear that trading the financial markets for a living is **not** easy. During the difficult times when I have made many painful losses the following quote by Mark Cook (one of the world's top financial market traders) has helped me:

"The true path to success always must journey through failure. All (and I mean all) the million dollar [income per year] traders I know had severe losses. And only when they coped with the losses did they achieve true success. The road is long - perhaps five to 10 years. The emotions will sometimes be an obstacle that just plain wins that battle. The true winner is the one who perseveres. The race is a marathon and not a sprint. Recognition that all humans fall short of perfect is the first step to the trek to knowing yourself and knowing your limitations. However, you must also keep foremost in mind that our God-given talents are very rarely realized to the true extent of the gift."

If you are interested in trading the financial markets, please download my Free 57 Page Trading Guide here:

www.TradingBook.net

Solomon Wealth Fund

In the five years January 2007 to December 2011 my average annual return on capital was 58.78% (i.e. per year).

The next logical step for me is to manage investors' funds. In order to learn about fund management, I started talking to the most successful people I could find in the industry. I have met with a number of very successful fund managers including one manager with over $20 billion under management and one with over $1.5 billion under management.

My most interesting discovery is that investors do not want outsized returns! The fund with $1.5 billion under management has averaged a return of 12% per annum since inception! The fund manager said to me that if I can consistently return 12 to 15% year after year with low volatility, investors will be very happy.

Needless to say a light went on in my head when I heard these stories! Investors would rather I consistently delivered 15% returns with low volatility (and therefore low risk) than 100% returns with the huge volatility I have been trading with.

I have therefore decided to lower the volatility and returns of the models I am using so the fund is more attractive to investors. Fortunately making the model less volatile is fairly simple because I can simply reduce leverage and reduce my position sizes, while still taking the entry and exits signals generated by my models.

You are welcome read about the fund which I plan to launch in the next year or two:

www.SolomonWealthFund.com

Please read the disclaimer on the site.

If you would like more information you can sign up on the site.

Chapter 10 - Peers and Peer Groups

You are the average of the five people you spend most of your time with.

Critical Principle 2:   **You are the average of the five people you spend most of your time with.**

It is absolutely essential to surround yourself with people who have the highest possible levels of integrity, energy, excellence, ability, joy, Godliness and so on. Look around! Who do you spend most of your time with? Workmates, friends, clients? Honestly evaluate whether your peers are taking you up, taking you down or keeping you where you are. If they are not taking you to higher levels, you **must** make a change.

If you are not married, put all of your energy into ensuring you only marry someone who will join you in a journey to higher, greater levels. If you are already married, your job is to lift your spouse to greater levels. Encourage your spouse to do the same for you.

Always surround yourself with positive people who are going places and living their dreams. Seriously consider taking a job that pays less but allows you to get close to people you really admire. Join a group that is full of the kinds of people who will challenge you to live life to the full. Find a mentor who has achieved what you want to achieve.

Life is too short to allow your peers to hold you back. And remember, you are someone else's peer too. Make sure you are encouraging and challenging those around you to higher and greater achievements.

I will give you a personal example. I like to exercise and go to the gym. I was working out two to three times a week with the same program for month after month, hardly making any progress. I met a personal trainer (Nira) at the gym who was bigger, stronger, and in much better shape than me. He had been a professional athlete and had a degree in sports science. I started working with him once a week. I have to tell you – he kicked my butt! I have never worked so hard in the gym. He pushed me and forced me to go beyond my limits, and I made huge progress in just a few weeks. Part of the motivation for me was just being around him. I didn't want to look like a weakling or a quitter, so I gave it everything I had. You have to find the best people you can to be your peers because their habits and ethos and wisdom rub off on you.

I particularly like Tony Robbins's summary:

"People's lives are a direct reflection of the expectations of their peer group."

Or more personally:

Your life is a direct reflection of the expectations of your peer group.

Think about that…

Your life is a direct reflection of the expectations of **your** peer group.

How to Find a Peer Group

If you recognize that you need new peers to challenge you to grow, this is how you go about it:

1. Identify One or Two Key Areas

You do not want to reinvent your whole peer group in one attempt. Pick one or two of the key areas in which you need to learn and grow and be challenged. If you have one area of your life you are completely passionate about, but you have no mentor or peer, choose that area. For example, you want to be a great guitar player, or an excellent marathon runner.

2. Identify Three or Four People

Find three or four people in that area who you can learn from and get inspiration from.

3. Model Them

Find out as much as you can about those people. Google them, visit them if you know them, find out what other people have said about them. See if there are articles or documentaries on them.

4. Follow Them

If they have blogs or are on Twitter or Facebook or have their own website, follow them to find out how they do what they do.

5. Absorb Their Teachings

If they have books, read them all. If they have CD and DVD courses, purchase them. If they run seminars, attend them.

6. Approach Them

No matter who they are, approach them. Write them a letter. See if you can email them. They are only human.

If you approach people in a way that makes them feel appreciated, you may be surprised how many people will positively respond to you.

7. Be Persistent

Without being a pest, be persistent. I will give you an example. I have had two situations where people have asked me if I will mentor them regularly. Although I gave each of them an hour one on one for nothing, I turned down their request because I have to be careful with my time. However I felt a bit guilty about it, and if they had come back to me once or twice more, asking again, I would almost certainly have worked something out for them.

8. Be Creative

In the next chapter I talk about how I used a creative approach to reach a celebrity, which turned out to be an amazing experience.

Most of the time you will not have to reach for the stars. Many times you can find peers in your own city or community whom you can approach. My personal trainer is a good example.

Be honest with yourself. Do you need to have more people around you who operate at a higher level than you do and who hold themselves to a higher standard? If so, start NOW to develop these new peers!

Action Step 3:

Identify one area of your life in which you need a high level peer. Identify two people who can be that peer. In the next 24 hours, make one simple step to start modeling that person for example order a book they have written or contact them.

Chapter 11 - The Mother of Creativity

In 1992 I started writing a Science Fiction novel *"The Simulan Game".* The book was written like a blockbuster movie, and my intention from the beginning was to turn it into a screenplay for an epic movie. So I decided to contact a movie director. One of the most brilliant screenwriters and directors of the last few years is Andrew Niccol.

I tried to contact him without success.

However I found that Andrew Niccol had not registered his own personal domain name. So I registered the domain name AndrewNiccol.com.

I set up a simple one page site (total cost under $50) which said this (I have shortened it here):

"Dear Andrew

I loved your movie "Lord of War" and I wanted to tell you personally.

Unfortunately I was unable to find any contact details for you whatsoever, so I hope you manage to find this!

I would like to talk about working with you on the screenplay of my novel, a futuristic thriller – The Simulan Game.

Please email me at _____.

Kind Regards

Oliver Hille
Mobile phone _____.

PS I am more than happy to give you your domain name!"

The website was up for over 4½ years, and I heard nothing!

However I had a written-down goal that I regularly affirmed and prayed out loud:

"My novel will become a bestseller and a movie."

And

"Lord please bless my novel to become a bestseller and a movie."

It was early September 2011, and I had not done these affirmations for quite a few weeks, but I did them on a Monday and Tuesday. Then on the Thursday of that week, I received an email from Andrew Niccol's assistant saying:

"Andrew would be more than happy to read your screenplay…"

She added that Andrew Niccol had a small window between movies to read my screenplay, and I needed to have it to him the week after next.

I have to emphasize that in my opinion Andrew Niccol is one of the greatest screenwriters of the last 20 years. He won an Oscar nomination for writing the screenplay for "The Truman Show" and wrote *and* directed both "Gattaca" and "Lord of War". Both "The Truman Show" and "Gattaca" were brilliantly original and insightful, and "Lord of War" has such clever and well written dialogue that I feel like I am in the presence of a master when I am watching it.

So obviously it was very exciting to think that this genius is going to read my screenplay.

However I had a number of problems:

1. My novel was less than half written.

2. I had never written a screenplay before, and I had no idea how to write one.

3. I did not know how to format a screenplay.

4. I was just a few weeks away from launching this book you are reading, and was very busy every day with that.

5. Because I had put all of my other projects on hold to launch this book, I was already earning no money (except my passive income) and writing a screenplay was another big project that I might never be paid for. And even if I did, it would be years until the movie was made and I got paid.

But of course I had just been handed a once in a lifetime opportunity, so I did the only thing I could do – I grabbed it with both hands.

Fortunately, some years before I had purchased the brilliant book "How to Write a Selling Screenplay" by Christopher Keane. However, it had sat in my bookshelf unread.

I started reading it. The first four chapters are about how to actually set about writing a screenplay. So I devoured those chapters first to get me in the right frame of mind.

Then I set about finishing my novel.

At that stage I had written 32,986 words so the novel was literally one third written (an average novel is around 100,000 words).

Now here is the interesting part: I started writing the novel in 1992, so it had embarrassingly taken me 19 years to write the first third. Guess what? Finishing the novel took me **five days**. Shame on me is all I can say.

I used to think that an hour a day of writing was something to celebrate. But in those five days, I only did three things: eat, sleep and write.

An amazing thing happened – I wrote with more energy, happiness and creativity than ever in my life before. Dialogue and concepts and ideas cascaded into my mind. Not for even one minute did I have a hesitation or "writers' block".

And when I wasn't writing, I had a smile on my face and a spring in my step – I was energized by the process.

Also because I generally sit in a chair at a computer for many hours a day, I sometimes get a sore back if I sit for too long. But this time I sat for twice as long every day and my back was fine!

So at the end of five days, I had a novel. But because it wasn't as good as I wanted it to be, I re-wrote it, changed it and improved it. Then I read through and edited it, and I had some new breakthrough ideas, and I re-wrote parts of it again. Finally I had a novel I was happy with. Now I needed to convert it into a screenplay.

I emailed Andrew Niccol's assistant to ask what font I should use. She told me that it was Courier 12pt but that Andrew Niccol used the industry standard screenwriting software "Final Draft". I didn't know there was such a thing as screenwriting software and I had never heard of "Final Draft". But I wanted to do the best possible job for Andrew Niccol so I knew I had to present him with my screenplay as a Final Draft document.

So in five marathon days, I purchased and downloaded Final Draft, learned how to use it, and I re-wrote my novel as a screenplay. Now that might sound easy but a screenplay is radically different to a novel. Assuming you don't use a voiceover (which I didn't) you cannot describe how a character feels or his/her motivations. That all has to be conveyed using a visual medium or character dialogue.

Also, a screenwriter has to explain in detail to the director what is happening in each scene e.g. where and at what time the scene takes place, where the camera is in relation to the characters, do we pan or zoom, use slow or normal film speed, etc. Also in a screenplay you have to describe everything in present tense whereas my novel is in past tense.

Fortunately I thought about my novel as a movie from when I first started writing it, so I knew how I wanted it to look and feel on screen. But even so, re-writing a scene for a screenplay can be complicated.

Also when you are re-writing from a novel to a screenplay, you go through everything in such detail that you naturally think of improvements and new ideas and better dialogue. So this became another full re-write.

When I finally finished the screenplay, five marathon days later, I sent a copy to my Dad to edit (God bless him – he did it in under 24 hours). Then I fully edited it again.

Finally after 15 days of non-stop writing, I emailed the screenplay to Andrew Niccol.

Although my back was fine, that night my legs were so sore from sitting in one place for nearly 200 hours in 15 days, that I could not sleep. I got up and checked on Google for the symptoms of Deep Vein Thrombosis (DVT)! Thankfully I did not have DVT but it took a few days for the pain to go away!

Even if nothing ever comes of it, I have learned some fantastic lessons that were worth all of my hard work.

Lesson 1: Creativity

"Deadlines are the Mother of Creativity."

I was presented with a deadline and a massive reward for completion. I did what I thought was inhumanly possible. But not only that, I was forced into a creative peak state. I didn't have to grind my way through it – the process energized me and the ideas literally jumped off my fingers.

It is almost certain that YOU have an unfinished creative project:

- Music;
- Art;
- Writing;
- Photography;
- Whatever.

I bet if someone credible walked up to you and said "I will give you $50,000 in cash if you complete your project in 30 days." you would do it – and it would be fantastic.

Somehow we need to force ourselves to have deadlines that really mean something to us. Here are some suggestions:

1. Make a commitment to me! Yes, I am willing to keep you accountable. Here is how.

Make your commitment on the following webpage:

www.LifestyleBook.com/my-commitment

This is a confidential commitment between you and me. Your commitment must include a date. I will email you on your commitment date to confirm.

Please note: This is a real commitment. By committing, you are giving me permission to **kick your butt** if you do not follow through. Please do not commit unless you are willing to put everything else aside to make your commitment come to pass.

You may also want to use this web page if you have already completed your project, but you have a fear of failure and you have not yet sent off your manuscript (or whatever you have done). For example, "I commit that I will post my novel off to a publisher within 14 days."

2. Commit to your own accountability group i.e. close friends or people you respect a lot.

3. Commit to someone that you will give $1,000 to an organization you are *against* if you do not meet your deadline.

4. Write to one of your idols in the relevant industry and tell them you will post your:

- Screenplay,
- Photo of your artwork,
- CD of your song,
- etc.

\-   to them within 30 days. That will force you to act.

Remember I had no idea what I was capable of until I was forced to act.

Lesson 2: Focus and Work Ethic

Writing 12 + hours a day is not like working in a factory or a corporate environment for 12 hours a day. I know, I have done all three. Creative writing is taxing on every level, especially with a multi-faceted novel. I considered it almost impossible to write for more than a few hours a day – but I was wrong.

Lesson 3: There is no such thing as "Writers' Block"

Okay I don't want to get myself in trouble with the millions of far more talented writers out there than me. And I am sure that many great writers had periods when the writing wouldn't come. But the great writers I have studied wrote every single day whether they felt like it or not, and whether they felt inspired or not.

I can tell you from this experience that I have never had so many ideas and been so creative. I now believe we all have a massive capacity for creativity that we are simply not tapping in to.

I believe we are all created in the image of God, and He has infinite creativity. It therefore follows that we too must be creative.

I believe that YOU are capable of achieving way more than you have ever dreamed.

If I believe in you and God believes in you, perhaps that is enough for you to take a leap of faith and reach for the stars in whatever it is you dream of achieving!

The name of my novel is "The Simulan Game." If you are interested in updates on what happens with my screenplay and my novel, including the launch of the novel, please sign up here:

www.TheSimulanGame.com

I have also written a comprehensive book on how to successfully self publish a book on Amazon:

"How to Become an Amazon #1 Bestselling Author – and Make Money!"

You can get a copy of the book here:

www.LifestyleBook.com/amazon

I also have a Free Webinar you can watch on YouTube re how to launch a book on Amazon. The video has thousands of views on YouTube. You can watch it here:

www.YouTube.com/watch?v=Zt4spXkpG8U

Chapter 12 - Finding Your Soul Mate

It is amazing how little advice is available, especially to young people, on choosing your soul mate or your spouse for life. On the other hand, there is a massive publishing industry built around resolving marital conflict, dealing with separation and divorce, keeping the love alive and so on.

Most of my married friends (and me included) consider there was a large amount of good fortune in their choice of our spouse. The reason is because none of us realized at the time what exactly we were agreeing to and how long "forever" really is! Neither did we realize how little we really knew about our spouses or ourselves on our wedding day! Of course some of our friends were not so fortunate and they are no longer together.

In fact a sad statistic is over one third of marriages end in divorce.

I suspect de-facto relationships have an even worse record.

My wife and I have been married for 19 years and I am delighted I decided to spend my life with her. In fact, I can honestly say I have not met anyone before or since that I would rather be married to. However, much of the reason for that is the blessing of God and good fortune.

Getting it right at the very start of a long-term relationship is critical if you want the best chance to avoid pain and frustration later on.

Here are the key factors in giving yourself the best chance of finding and staying with a soul-mate and life partner:

1. Understand Yourself

You cannot hope to find the right person if you don't know who you are and where you are heading. Invest time in finding out what really makes you excited and holds your attention. Work out what you believe and why. Until you get to that point, don't dream of making a life-long commitment to someone else!

I have a friend who was always attracted to "victims" i.e. people who were broken in some way and needed help. This woman started to date these types of men. I told her I believed that one of her gifts was to reach out to broken people and to help them, but she shouldn't necessarily look for brokenness in a life partner. She did end up marrying someone who needed help, and yes he is a lucky guy. But it is not an ideal situation for her, and I believe it has compromised her ability to use her gift. Had she married a strong, well-centered man, they would have had a life that would have allowed her to fully utilize her gift. As it is, they lead quite separate lives, and many of her early dreams of helping others have been suffocated.

2. Understand Your Partner

It is so easy in the beginning to see all the similarities you share. Someone likes you and you like them. Their voice sounds like beautiful music, and their smile lights up the room. You daydream about them all day long and you start writing poetry! But STOP! That isn't enough to base a lifetime commitment on. You need to really and truly get to know and understand that person. Anyone can pretend to be anything they want to be for a few months and both parties are always on their best behavior for the first few months.

You need to ask your partner the big questions of life, their dreams and aspirations. You should get them to read your favorite books and you should read theirs. Attend seminars together. Don't ignore or gloss over differences and annoyances. Small problems in relationships tend to become monsters after you get married!

3. Influences

Everyone is the average of the five people they spend the most time with. Who are their closest friends? Who are their role-models? Who are their heroes or heroines? That is what they are really like and what they are gravitating towards.

4. Your Partner's Parents

There is no avoiding that your partner is genetically 50% of each of his/her parents. Not only that, but they have also been shaped and socialized by those parents. The more you get to know your partner the more you will realize that in a huge number of ways they are a half-twin of each of their parents. The practical reality is that you had better really like your partner's parents because your partner is going to strongly resemble them when they are that age!

5. Similarity Breeds Content

It is simple but it is true, the more you have in common the happier and more content you will be. The psychology literature and research agrees. For example *"greater similarity between partner was associated with higher levels of marital satisfaction"* (Journal of Personality, Volume 74(5), 2006, p1401).

If you write down your core beliefs and core values and favorite pastimes and most important activities, these *must* be broadly the same as those of your partner. Even non-critical issues can be very important. If for example you like to exercise in your spare time, and your partner likes to eat junk food in front of the TV, you will make new exercise friends and start to move in a different direction to your partner. More importantly you should understand your partner's views on money *before* you have a joint bank account. You should find out their ideas on parenthood *before* you become parents.

If you find you really don't have much in common when it comes to the important things in life, it is much better to walk away now rather than be trapped with someone you have no common ground with.

6. Beauty is Skin Deep

Okay it is important that you are "hot" for your partner, and you think they are beautiful and sexy. But that on its own is not enough. In fact in the first few months it can get in the way of really finding out about your partner. Their beauty can blind you to their faults or make you gloss-over the attributes you don't like. Make sure you don't make a life-long commitment to someone when you are in this space. Take a step back and imagine they are very plain looking. Beauty is only skin deep and it becomes irrelevant if you don't also love the person inside.

Practical Steps

If you have not already found your soul mate here are some powerful practical steps to enable you to find the right person:

1. Write a List of Wants

Get a new exercise book and write down all of the wants and must-haves of the person you are looking for. Be as specific as possible. Give as much detail as possible. Imagine your perfect match and write down everything about them. It is a good idea to add pictures into your book, not only of what they look like but pictures of your future life together.

2. Write a list of Must Nots

Then write a list of all of the things your soul mate must not be. All of the habits, attributes, and attitudes you don't want them to have. Once again give details and be specific. If you can't stand people who answer their mobile phone during dinner, write it down!

3. Most Important

Once you have completed points one and two, in a separate part of the exercise book write down a detailed answer to the following question:

What do I have to do and be in order to attract that person into my life?

Let's be honest for a minute. If you have just described a near perfect human being with a sparkling personality and every wonderful gift, are they going to be interested in **you**? If you settle for mediocrity, don't care much about your appearance, have a host of bad habits are you going to attract your dream soul mate?

The most important part of this exercise is to ensure you are worthy of the soul mate of your dreams. If you are not there yet, it is time for you to go to work on **you**.

4. Pray

It is impossible to over emphasise how important it is to find the right spouse. They will be the other parent to your children, your friend, your intimate lover, your support and so on. Regardless of your theology I thoroughly recommend you pray, meditate and then listen to God and to your own heart before making a lifelong commitment. When friends ask me for advice in this area I always tell them to fast and pray and listen for three full days. It is too important a decision to leave to your emotions and your hopes.

5. Reading and Courses

There are a lot of good books and courses on relationships. Two I have found especially good are:

- The book "Men are From Mars, Women are From Venus" by John Gray.

- The CD and DVD series by Tony and Sage Robbins "Love and Passion Ultimate Relationship Program".

Chapter 13 - Children

If you are unable to have children or you have made a definite decision not to have children, please skip this chapter.

On the face of it, having children might look like the worst lifestyle choice you can make. They take up a huge amount of your most precious asset (time), they cost a lot of money, you will need a bigger house, and you may even need a totally un-cool people-mover! But the reality is different. Unless you simply can't stand kids, having children is the best lifestyle choice you can make.

Children are without any doubt the best thing in the world.

Critical Principle 3: **Children are the best thing in the world.**

I have never experienced anywhere near the joy, the laughter, the fun, the love and the natural high my children give me. Before I had children I really loved life but looking back it was nowhere near as rich and full and wonderful as it is now with our three beautiful children. This is not just my opinion. It is a sentiment shared by all of my friends who have kids.

It is impossible to convey what it means to be a parent to someone who has never had children, but this chapter will help you plan your future if you intend to have children, or already have them.

I sometimes wonder why no-one told me how great it was to have kids. I think one reason is that in previous generations the father was not encouraged to be involved like fathers are today. Often they were the breadwinner and the disciplinarian, and they were expected to be somewhat distant from their children. This distance from the start did not allow fathers to bond deeply with their children, and the distance was then harder to bridge. Today's Dads are totally different. We get to bond immediately with a new baby at the same time as Mom does. We are encouraged to touch and cuddle and play with our babies. That bond is easy to maintain and a positive cycle begins.

Mothers of course have always had that close bond with their children. However, in previous generations much of motherhood was hard physical work, often with not much money coming in and with the father helping very little. Imagine keeping a busy household going without automatic washing machines, dishwashers, vacuum cleaners, a second car, etc. Consequently mothers of previous generations were worked ragged and often didn't have the time and energy we can enjoy today.

Further, the Victorian attitude to parenting was to encourage distance from children, emotional detachment, and it emphasised discipline and respect. That attitude can still be found to some extent today. I'm sure you have heard:

> "Children should be seen and not heard."
> "Keep a stiff upper lip."
> "Big boys don't cry."
> "Nice ladies play quietly."

But the good news is we can ignore those negative Victorian standards. We can smother our kids with hugs, kisses, love, fun, laughter and positive words. We can bathe with them, snuggle up in bed with them, play-fight with them, tickle them, role-play with them, sing to them, do magic tricks with them, roly-poly with them, stare at the stars with them – whatever. We have a wonderful freedom to re-live our childhood by acting as a kid with them – something the Edwardians and Victorians could never do.

Warning – I don't want to give you the impression that being a parent is easy and simple. In fact, being a parent is hard work and sometimes exhausting. It can't be fun all of the time. There are parts that are mundane and frustrating and scary. Also, it is no place for selfishness. You learn to be selfless and you put the needs (and wants!) of your kids ahead of yourself. Newspapers don't get read, cups of tea don't get finished, and sleeping through the night becomes a happy memory of times past. The point is, the highs far outweigh the lows, and the hard work is forgotten with one smile or cuddle or "I love you daddy."

For children to really enhance your lifestyle there are a number of things to get right. If you don't get them right, you will suffer and your kids will suffer:

1. Plan First

If you are yet to have children but you expect to, it is critical that you plan for their arrival. There are two things you need to plan for: time and money.

(a) Time

Because kids are so great, you want to spend lots and lots of time with them. I never realized this and nor did my peers. Believe me when I say that once you have a new baby, the idea of working long hours or travelling with work loses its appeal in a hurry. Similarly, if you think you and your partner will want to work full time after the maternity/paternity period, then be prepared for a surprise. Most new parents I know really want one parent to be home with the children either full time or part time. Unfortunately, financial necessity often requires both parents to work full time.

It is also great to be able to take time for your kids during the week for example baby's first health check-up, first day of preschool, sports day, swimming sports, school concerts etc.

One of my favorite summer lunch times is when it is a sunny day, I will surprise my kids by turning up to school at lunch time. We sit and have lunch together, and then we walk around the playground together hand in hand – we all love it. I couldn't do this if I worked in an office in town. I see my kids off to school in the morning, and I see them when they come home from school. This gives me a lot of time at both ends of the day to play and interact with my kids.

Sadly, statistics tell us that most fathers spend around ten minutes per **week,** one on one interacting with their kids. In this scenario everyone misses wonderful hours of golden moments. Some parents try to cover up this lack by talking about "quality time". They argue that spending half an hour of scheduled quality time is nearly as good as spending a lot of unstructured time with children. This is just conscience-salvaging rubbish. Time and lots of it is what kids need. And clearly, being in the same room as kids when they are watching TV is not spending time with them.

So given that you will want to and you will need to spend a lot of time with your kids, you need to plan for that before they arrive. Aim to have a job or a business that is flexible enough to allow you to take the time to be with your kids.

(b) Money

There is no question that kids cost money. Firstly, there are the obvious costs such as baby formula, nappies, clothes, toys etc. And then the hidden costs like bigger houses and cars. Also of course time is money, and if one parent quits a job or goes down to part time, there will be a huge decrease in income. Even if both parents work full time, the childcare costs are huge. If you have not planned for these costs they will really hit you.

A number of years ago, we had friends who lived it up before their kids arrived. They had two nice incomes and they rented a cheap house. Every fortnightly pay-day the woman would buy a new outfit. The man bought all sorts of toys. They spent money like water. They lived like kings until their first baby arrived. Then suddenly they lost her income, had to move house, and had baby expenses. Within a couple of months they were on the bones of their butts, totally broke, living from one pay packet to the next. This put huge strain on the family and on their marriage and made their day to day life very difficult. The flash outfits were now worthless, and the woman had nowhere to wear them. The guy's toys had devalued, and he had less time to play with them. If only they had planned ahead, their family life would have been so much more fulfilling and enjoyable and stress free.

My advice is save hard two to three years before you have kids and don't make commitments (for example a huge mortgage) that make you broke when you have children.

2. Bonding

Bonding with your kids starts the moment they are born and even before in utero. For Dad's if you possibly can, take two weeks off as soon as your baby is born. This is a critical time in the bonding process. After that take every opportunity to hug, kiss, bath and play with your kids. It is my experience that hands-on parents get the most out of being a parent.

3. Be a kid

I know this is easier for some people than others. Luckily for me, acting like a kid is fun. Role plays and games and rolling around on the floor is as much fun for me as it is for my kids. But if you can find some activities you like as much as they do, concentrate on those. For example, I don't like sitting at a table doing finger-painting or paper mache – but some parents love it. Find those things both you and your kids love, get on their level and go crazy doing it. It can be just like having a second childhood. I especially enjoy buying all the toys I never had as a kid and always wanted – like radio controlled cars. I recently sneaked off with a friend I went to primary school with, and we played with the radio controlled cars – we laughed like ten year olds!

4. Words

Kids love to be told how great they are and how much you love them. So tell them all the time! Encourage them, praise them and tell them all the great things that make them special.

From my experience if you follow these guidelines, you will start and maintain great relationships with your kids. This in turn will help to make the best lifestyle choice you can make (having kids), all the more enjoyable.

Chapter 14 - Sleep

Fifty years ago people in the West slept an average of nine hours a night. Fifteen years ago we slept eight hours a night. But now we average seven hours of sleep a night.

There is quite a lot of research quoted in this chapter because I want to convince you just how important sleep is.

A 2001 poll taken by the American National Sleep Foundation (NSF) reported that 63 percent of American adults did not receive the recommended eight hours of sleep necessary for good health, safety and optimum performance.[1]

The research recommends we have an average of eight hours sleep every night. Clearly everyone is different and we all have slightly different sleep needs. But if you do not get the sleep you need you become sleep-deprived.

Sleep deprivation causes the following:

1. Fatigue

Fatigue's consequences include higher instances of motor vehicle accidents, work-related accidents, decreased productivity and adverse health effects. Daniel O'Hearn, a Johns Hopkins University sleep disorders specialist observed, *"People don't respect sleep enough. They feel they can do more - have more time for work and family - by allowing themselves less time for sleep".*[2]

2. Poor Health

A 2001 Sleep Foundation survey draws attention to several medical conditions linked directly to sleep deprivation, including depression (83 percent), night time heartburn (82 percent), diabetes (81 percent), hypertension (79 percent), and heart disease (78 percent). In addition, sleep deprivation can accelerate the aging process, lead to obesity and increase the risk of memory loss. The British Medical Association also confirmed higher levels of stress, anxiety and depression among the sleep-deprived.[3]

3. Poor Wealth

According to Cornell University psychologist and sleep expert James Maas, sleep deprivation and sleep disorders cost the American economy at least $150 billion a year, as a result of decreased job productivity and fatigue-related accidents.[4]

Sleep researcher Eve van Cauter at the University of Chicago exposed sleep-deprived students (allowed only four hours per night for six nights) to flu vaccine; their immune systems produced only half the normal number of antibodies in response to the virus. Levels of cortisol (a hormone associated with stress) rose, and the sympathetic nervous system became active, raising heart rates and blood pressure. The subjects also showed insulin resistance, a pre-diabetic condition that affects glucose tolerance and produces weight gain.

So those are the negatives of a poor sleep. What are the benefits of a good sleep?

Two key benefits of having a good sleep are:

1. It Boosts Your Immune System

Researchers in Germany found that among a group of volunteers vaccinated against hepatitis A infection, those who got a good night's sleep afterwards showed a stronger immune response to the vaccine.[5]

2. It Improves Longevity

Sleeping well helps keep you alive longer. Among humans, death from all causes is lowest among adults who get seven to eight hours of sleep nightly, and significantly higher among those who sleep less than seven hours.[6]

I have the type of personality that likes to push boundaries, and I like to get the most out of every day. Because of this I have often not slept enough. In my late twenties I was working hard as an accountant, plus doing tax returns for private clients, and also building up a property portfolio, so I was busy all week long. I found that in general I could get by on six hours sleep a night and could even manage the occasional night of only four hours sleep. After about a year of this I could feel my stress levels rising. Sometimes I was so stressed that when I went to bed at night I wondered (irrationally) whether I would actually wake up in the morning, or die in my sleep. I got sick often and enjoyed life less. I finally went to the doctor who quizzed me on my lifestyle. He told me I had to make changes to my lifestyle or things would get worse. I immediately cut down on the extra work I was doing and made some changes. It took about six months to get back to feeling normal and I have learned my lesson.

There was one exception. In the late 90s I was working as an accountant in London, working 50-hour weeks plus a two-hour commute every day. I knew I was getting tired and stressed but I decided (foolishly) to see how far I could push myself. So I worked longer and harder, and one day I was so tired I fell asleep at work sitting on the toilet! Soon after that I got shingles which is pretty awful, and I had to take two weeks off work (unpaid). So I found out my limit, and I paid for it. It took me about three months to get to 100% energy again.

About two years ago I made a conscious decision to get at least seven and a half hours sleep a night and more if I felt tired. The result is that I have far more energy and enthusiasm, and I get sick a lot less.

If you can't free up any more time in your day for sleep then you need to make a lifestyle change. It might be as simple as no more TV, DVD's and movies!

Note: See my discussion on Caffeine in the chapter "Exercise and Diet" on how caffeine intake can negatively impact your sleep.

Footnotes:

1. National Sleep Foundation "Less Fun, Less Sleep, More Work: An American Portrait." Mar. 27, 2001.
2. FDA Consumer Magazine. "Sleepless Society" July-August 1998.
3. "Sleep Deprivation as Bad as Alcohol Impairment, Study Suggests." CNN Health. Sept 20, 2000.
4. "National Sleep Debt is Killing Americans and Hurting Economy", Cornell Psychologist, Jan. 19, 1998.
5. Journal of Psychosomatic Medicine Sept/Oct 2003.
6. www.harvardmagazine.com "Deep into Sleep" by Craig Lambert.

Chapter 15 - Personal Finances 101

I was trained as a Chartered Accountant (CPA), and I still hold that qualification. I also have a first class honours degree in accountancy, and I lecture accounting at university. So you could say I was well qualified to give advice on accounting.

However, what you are taught in:

- School accounting classes;
- Small business classes;
- University accounting classes; and
- On the job accounting and book keeping;

is almost exactly the opposite of what you and I need to know about our own personal finances.

Let me give you an example. In traditional accounting, anything that has a current or future value is an asset. So if a company owns a car it is recognized and accounted for as an asset, because it is worth something. On the other hand a liability is anything that requires a current or future payment. Assets are accounted for as positive numbers and liabilities as negative numbers. That is all very well for a company but for an individual you must think a completely different way. This might be a little more difficult for people with accounting or book keeping backgrounds but once you get it, you can make the mental shift in seconds, just like I did.

For you and I accounting for our own personal finances is simple:

A real asset is anything that:

- Puts money into your bank account; or

- Increases in value; or
- Is cash; or
- A cash equivalent.

A liability is anything that takes money out of your bank account.

It sounds simple doesn't it? So you shouldn't be surprised when I tell you:

- Your car is a liability.
- Your home is a liability.
- Your boat is a liability.
- Your vacation house is a liability.
- Your TV is a liability.
- Your pool is a liability.
- Your mobile phone is a liability.
- Your pet is a liability.
- Your household furniture and furnishings are a liability.
- Your hobbies are a liability.
- Your vacations are a liability.

All of these cost you money. They all take money out of your bank account. Even if some of them don't do it every week (for example your furniture), they all need to be replaced, so over time they cost you money.

It is vitally important we realize these are real liabilities that are causing huge amounts of money to disappear from our lives. You might rightly argue that some of these are necessary for living and I agree with you. But almost everyone in the industrialized world falls into the trap of buying bigger and more expensive things than they need. In addition, many people acquire a lot of other paraphernalia they don't need at all. Some of these "assets" are fun to own but most of us forget they are all liabilities that suck money away from us. You only get to spend money once!

Let's look at a practical example:

Bob and Sue realize after doing a budget that the cash they have available after they have deducted all of their living expenses is $26,000 per year. Out of this $26,000 they need to deduct their house and car expenses.

Bob and Sue own two cars worth $10,000 each and their home is nicely furnished. The actual money flowing out of Bob and Sue's bank account for these items in one year is:

Mortgage $200,000 at 4%	$8,000
Car loans $10,000 at 5%	$500
Car maintenance, insurance and depreciation	$2,000
Furniture depreciation	$1,000
Total	$11,500

The ideal decision right now is to invest the extra $14,500 excess cash i.e.:

$26,000
-$11,500
$14,500

Bob and Sue should invest this money every year into Real Assets that put additional money into their annual income – simple! Then their annual income continues to grow and not only grow but compound.

"The most powerful force in the universe is compound interest."
Albert Einstein

Critical Principle 4:   **Compounding your wealth is the most effective way to get rich slowly.**

If we use a 5% real return on the original $14,500 and Bob and Sue continue to put $14,500 every year into Real Assets (on a monthly basis), after 10 years they will have $211,514! This is without increasing the monthly payments i.e. this does not include increased salaries or inheritances etc.

Taken further, assume Bob and Sue are 30 years from retirement. Saving $14,500 per year in the same way gives an inflation adjusted total of just over $1,000,000! Bear in mind this is based on a conservative rate of return of only 5% per year. So why aren't there relaxed millionaires everywhere you look? The reason is simple! The Bob and Sues of the world do the opposite! They buy what traditional accounting calls assets but are actually liabilities. What most Bob and Sues do is look at their annual excess of $14,500 and they do the following:

Buy a new house with a pool that costs $125,000 more than the old house, buy new furniture for the house, upgrade both cars and buy a boat.

Now their outgoings are:

Mortgage $352,000 at 4%	$13,000
Car loans $40,000 at 5%	2,000
Car maintenance, insurance and depreciation	4,000
New furniture depreciation	3,000
Boat maintenance and depreciation	2,000
Pool maintenance	1,000
Total	$26,000

Now Bob and Sue are keeping up with the Joneses but the problem is the Joneses (and almost everyone else) are spiralling into a poverty trap. What is worse, every five or ten years as their salaries increase Bob and Sue upgrade everything again so they never have any Real Assets. This is why most people never achieve financial independence.

Remember Real Assets are assets that put money into your bank account. There are really only five classes of Real Assets:

- Your own business.
- Real estate.
- Equities (stocks).
- Interest Bearing (for example bank deposits, treasury bills).
- Liquid commodities (i.e. commodities that can be turned instantly into cash for example gold).

If you really understand this chapter and put into practice only spending your excess cash on Real Assets, in 10, 20 or 30 years you will be wealthier than 90% of the people around you. If you are in the position where you have no excess cash, chances are it's because in the past you have spent your excess cash on liabilities and upgrading. If you are serious about being independently wealthy I suggest you spend the next five minutes completing your own (or your family) Personal Real Balance Sheet and your own Personal Real Budget.

Write down your current financial position below:

Personal Real Balance Sheet

Real Assets **(Put $ in my bank)**	**Real Liabilities** **(Take $ out of my bank)**
Equities/stocks Bank deposits and similar Profitable businesses Real estate investments Liquid commodities	(see the list of expenses next two pages)

Personal Real Budget

Weekly Net Income (Salary, Interest, Rent, Business Income, Dividends, Royalties etc)

Less Weekly Expenses

Groceries
Gifts
Clothing – Adults
Clothing - Kids
Presents for Kids
Presents for Us
Presents for Others
Cleaner
Take Out Food
Eating at Restaurants
Cars - Insurance and Taxes
Car Maintenance and Service (for each car)
Petrol/Diesel all Cars
Boat or other Recreational Expenses
Property Taxes
Mortgage
Property Insurance
Contents Insurance
Life Insurance
Health Insurance
Gym Membership
Magazine Subscriptions
Vacations
Tithing
Other Giving
Electricity
Home Phone
Mobile Phones
Entertainment
Cafes
Lunches

Haircuts
Alcohol
Section Maintenance
Babysitters
Pool Maintenance
Other (could be a number of other expenses not listed above)

You may be shocked to find that you have zero or very few Real Assets. In that case, today is the day you had a revelation of how to become independently rich.

Start by deciding not to upgrade where you don't need to. Don't "spend up large" when you don't need to. Don't "splash out" or "max out the credit card" or take an expensive vacation. These can all wait until you are independently wealthy. Next look for ways you can downsize. Downsize you house (i.e. your mortgage), downsize your car, downsize your expensive hobbies and toys. All of these "nice to haves" can wait until you are independently wealthy.

You may also be surprised just how much you are spending on "living". Unless you already live very frugally you can easily cut 10% of your monthly expenses.

I want to finish with a wonderful example of someone who took these principles to heart from a young age:

John Marks Templeton

When John Templeton and his wife married, they made a resolution to save 50% of every pay check they received. In addition they gave away a tithe (10%). They lived only on the 40%. John Templeton was 25 years old and not earning much. They also had a rule that their rent could not be more than 16% of the money they had left over after they had paid taxes their tithe and their 50% investment i.e. rent was 16% of 40% = 6.4% of their total income. They furnished their property with very cheap second hand furniture. Templeton also furnished his early offices with second hand furniture. He never had a credit card, and he never had a mortgage (he later always paid cash for his properties). At the time of his death in 2008, he was a self made **Billionaire**. He attributes a great deal of his wealth to his thrift and his belief in the power of compounding interest.

I recommend his wonderful book, "The Templeton Plan".

To illustrate his point on compound interest, here is a quote from his book:

"In history we're taught that the Indians were foolish to sell Manhattan for so little [beads worth $24]. But if you look at the reality of compound interest you'll find that if the Indians had invested their money at 8 percent interest at the time of the sale, they would now have $11 trillion. That is more than the value of all the real estate in the entire Western Hemisphere today!"

That was written in 1987. Compounding at the same rate until 2012 this would amount to over $65 trillion.

Chapter 16 - Pay Yourself First

I am embarrassed to say that I learned this lesson only in the last couple of years. If I had learned this lesson when I was 20, my wealth would be more than a million dollars greater than it is today.

Most of us have been socialized and modeled financial behavior that does **not** lead to wealth creation. The typical pattern is this:

Receive Money

Pay living expenses

See what is left over

Spend what is left over

Perhaps put a tiny amount aside for retirement

Let's stop and think about how well this model works. When you look around at people who are 40 years old and older, do you see many people getting a lot wealthier, having more time, having less financial stress, and some deciding to stop working because their passive income is so high? No! You usually see the opposite.

But there are a small percentage of people who have deliberately rejected the common model and have done something radical:

The paid themselves **first**.

Okay, so what does this mean?

It simply means that their model works like this:

Receive Money

Take a large percentage of that money and invest it, and **never** use the money for anything else

See what is left over

Spend what is left over on living expenses

If you apply this model to your life, in 20 years you will be wealthier than 99% of all the people you know.

How do I know? Because this is how billionaires like Warren Buffett, J. Paul Getty and Sir John Templeton became billionaires.

As I said earlier, Sir John Templeton's investment percentage was 50% even when he was just starting out and was broke. 50% is a huge percentage (work out half of your salary/wages and imagine investing that amount every week). But if you are determined you can do it.

Let's be more conservative and say you put aside and invest 25% of your income.

Simple Example

After tax income $52,000 per year = $1,000 per week

25% of $1,000 = $250 per week – you invest this amount.
Working with a 6% annual return after inflation, at the end of 20 years your investment is worth:

$506,905 (inflation adjusted)

At the end of 30 years your investment is worth:

$1,089,421 (inflation adjusted)

And this is without increasing your weekly amount of $250. So the figures above are conservative because as your salary increases, your investment amount increases. You would also add 25% of any windfalls such as an inheritance.

So look around at people who have been earning for 30 years. How many of them have over $1,000,000 in investments (excluding their family home)?

Imagine if they **did** have $1m in investments earning 6% per year. That would be $60,000 every year in passive income.

What kind of Lifestyle could you live if you had $60,000 passive income coming in every year?

That person can and must be you. No matter how old you are, start this week.

But you will have to have a mind shift and you will have to change your model.

You will most likely have to start living on less than you are used to, right now.

You might have to downsize your life for a while. But the benefit will be HUGE.

From now on, live a new more powerful, more wealthy way:

Pay yourself FIRST!

Chapter 17 - Compounding

"The most powerful force is the universe is compound interest."
Albert Einstein

One of my favorite definitions of wealth is the transfer of money from the impatient to the patient. Compound interest is the ultimate super weapon of the patient.

Consider this: if you had invested $1 at the time of Jesus birth, at the rate of 3% per year compounding, your investment would today be worth more than every asset on earth including real estate, precious metals, commodities, diamonds and cash.

In fact here is the actual amount of money you would have after 2,000 years:

$45,878,814,326,049,600,000,000,000

For comparison this is one trillion dollars:

$1,000,000,000,000

Of course no-one has a 2,000 year investment time horizon, but how about 45 years?

Warren Buffett has averaged a 20.3% return since he purchased Berkshire Hathaway in 1965.

So what if a relative of yours had invested $100,000 with Warren Buffett in 1965?

Today it would be worth $492 million.

$492,000,000

Of course it is only with hindsight that we can pick the best investor the world has ever known, but the principle is the key.

Let's look at a more reasonable example. If a relative of yours had invested $100,000 in the S&P500 (broad US stock market index) in 1950, today (adjusted for inflation) you would have $6,200,000.

So practically what does all of this mean?

As I said in the "Pay Yourself First" chapter, start right now to take the first 10%, 20% or more of your earnings and invest that amount in an asset class that has a history of making a return significantly above inflation. If you want to help yourself in the future start putting money aside. If you want to help your children or your grandchildren, start a fund for them.

If you receive a windfall from the sale of a business, or a rental property, or an inheritance, put aside a large portion of that as a compounding investment.

This is a sure way to grow your wealth.

Chapter 18 - Passive Income

You could say the Holy Grail of maximising the ratio of income earned to time expended is passive income. In its simplest form, passive income is when money comes in regardless of whether you are asleep, on vacation, or in a coma. Its close cousin is semi-passive income which is when money comes in all on its own, but you have to do a little bit of work now and then to keep it coming.

The best examples of purely passive income are:

- Interest on bank deposits or similar;
- Dividends on equities (stocks);
- Royalties on published books or music or software;
- Income from a website that automatically sells an electronic product or service.

The best examples of semi-passive income are:

- Rent from property;
- An investment in a business where you are a silent (not involved) partner;
- Almost fully automated businesses, especially web based.

From a lifestyle point of view, you should be aiming to derive as much passive and semi-passive income as possible, for the simple reason that it preserves your most valuable asset – your time.

Take a couple of minutes to think about and write down in the space below how your current hobby, passion or business interest could be made into an opportunity for passive or semi-passive income.

More Money, More Time

Most people associate their time with their ability to make money i.e. "If I work harder I will make more". We have to stop thinking like that and start to recognize that the best way to maximise making money but minimise time spent is to:

- Plan everything out at the start.
- Spend some time at the beginning.
- Make money for a long period thereafter without putting in any (or very little) time.

Let's take a couple of simple examples:

1. You decide to buy a rental property. All of the hard work is done at the beginning. You spend some weeks finding the best property, you negotiate, you do the legal stuff, perhaps you do some renovations, find great tenants, draw up the contracts, and then the bulk of the work is done. You then collect the rent.

2. You decide to set up a website with great content for mountain bikers. You do the research on websites, you find great content, you pay someone to build the site for you, you find some advertisers or use Google Ads, and the hard work is done. You then collect the advertising revenue.

Most of us started out as employees, whether it was a paper round or a summer job or a graduate position. We have been programmed to believe that the way to earn more is to work more. Even salaried positions have an implication that the more senior you are the more hours you have to work. This is the opposite of the way an entrepreneur has to think.

Once again, take a moment to stop and think about how you have been socialized to believe that your income is dependent on the time you expend. Then specifically reject that model and start brainstorming ways you can turn your passion into:

- Making a Plan;
- Doing some hard work at the beginning;
- Setting up an income stream that requires little or no oversight.

Chapter 19 - Double Your Income

This chapter is specifically written for people who are employees and whose income is under $50,000 p.a. However the principles apply regardless of your income and are even more powerful if you are under-employed or a student. If none of these apply to you, you may want to skip this chapter.

If I said you could **double** your income either by taking certain opportunities or by working 15% more, would you would be interested?

Let's look at an example to see how this is easily achievable:

Let's say Jane Smith's annual gross (before tax) income is $35,000. Assume her tax will be $6,825 leaving her $28,175

$28,175 / 52 = $540 per week

Jane's weekly expenses are:

Food per week	100
Rent	100
Flat expenses	20
Petrol	30
Clothing	20
Presents for Others	10
Take Out Food	10
Eating Out	10
Lunches	20
Car - Insurance and Rego	10
Car Maintenance	10
Gym	15
Vacations	10
Phone	10
Entertainment	40
Cafes	20
Other	15
Total	**450**

This leaves Jane $90 per week to save or put towards something other than living that week. This $90 is Jane's real income. The rest she spends on just living. Therefore, for Jane to double her real income all she needs to do is earn another $90 a week.

Here are a number of ways Jane can earn another $90 a week:

1.   Ask for a raise

If Jane has been at her job at least nine months she could approach her employer and say she wants a pay rise of $5,500 per year. She could make it clear to her employer that she is willing to take on more responsibility and a few extra hours.

It does take courage to ask but the worst that can happen is the employer says "No". If it is easier you can put the request in writing. A good employer will not mind being asked.

2.   Change jobs

If Jane's request for a pay increase is not accepted, she could look at changing jobs. It is usually easier to get promoted by changing jobs. If it is a professional position you should have worked for your current employer for at least two years. If it is a casual position you can leave at any time.

3.   Start a home-based business

Jane could use some of her spare time to start a low-cost home business. She should concentrate on her passions and interests. If she is stuck for ideas she should at least start trying to buy some items cheaply and re-sell them on an auction site for a profit.

4.   Find a part-time job

Remember Jane only has to earn $90 a week after tax to double her real income. It is not difficult to find weekend or evening work.

Once again, go with your passions and interests. If you love coffee, approach your favorite café and tell them you are looking for part-time work. If you love art, approach a gallery or art shop. If you love farming, contact some farmers.

If you get stuck try working earlier mornings in a bakery, or pumping gas or whatever. Remember you are doubling your real income.

When I was a student I cleaned a supermarket from 6am to 8am every morning. It wasn't easy getting up at 5am but every week I put money into my bank and my student friends only took money out. Then later on when my student friends were broke, I bought a Fender Stratocaster (electric guitar).

Chapter 20 - Only Buy What You Can Afford

As I said earlier, one of my favorite definitions of wealth is:

The transfer of money from the impatient to the patient.

Too often we try to acquire things now that we cannot really afford. If you have paid interest on your credit card, or borrowed to buy a car, or have made purchases on an installment plan, then this is you!

If you want to get ahead financially, you should only buy things you can afford now. It boils down to this:

If you can't pay cash for it now, don't buy it.

Example 1: You want to buy a car, and you have saved $1,000.

Option 1: You could use the $1,000 as a deposit on a $7,000 car. But then you have a $6,000 debt at high interest which is going to drain your cash flow for a year or two or more. Also because cars depreciate (go down in value) quickly, you will end up in a situation in a couple of years where you own a car worth $4,000 with a debt of $4,500 and your $1,000 deposit is gone. Financial suicide!

Option 2: You buy a car worth $1,000 and drive it until you have saved enough for an upgrade.

Option 3: If you can't find a car that suits you for $1,000, take public transport until you have saved enough.

Personal example: At the end of 1997 my salary was $38,000 and my wife's salary was $30,000. We had managed to buy four properties with a combined value of $1.2 million. However, we had very little cash, and we had one car – a 1984 Honda CRX worth $700.

Example 2: You want to buy domestic appliances and a new TV.

Option 1: You buy them all new via installment plan. This costs you $4,000. You have to pay an upfront fee, and interest, and your cash-flow is drained for the next five years.

Option 2: You spend $600 and buy everything second-hand

Example 3: Some friends invite you to go on vacation. The cost including shopping and hotels will be $1,500.

Option 1: You pay for everything on your credit card, and it is two years before you pay it off.

Option 2: You either save the money, or you don't go. It hurts for one year, after that you will be better off. In fact you could afford to go, and your friends on the same budget couldn't.

Example 4: Spring Shopping Spree.

Option 1: You buy yourself some new summer clothes for $1,000. You don't have the money now, so you put it on your credit card.

Option 2: You know you have $40 a week for clothes (because you have done your budget). You buy one item of clothing every fortnight on payday with the excess cash you have.

Option 3: Re-think your priorities. Do you really need to spend $500-$1,000 on clothes? A couple of select items and making do with what you have would be a better use of your precious cash.

If you are serious about getting ahead financially in the long run, here are my "Ensure You Are Wealthy Later" Tips:

Tip#1: Never borrow to buy a car.

Tip#2: Never take on an installment plan (hire purchase) to buy something.

Tip#3: Never use your credit card unless you have that amount in your bank or spare in your next pay packet.

Tip#4: Cut up your credit cards if the spending power is too tempting.

Tip#5: Never get sucked in by advertisements that say "24 months to pay" or "no deposit".

When it is okay to borrow money:

1. To buy your own property.

2. To buy something you can make a financial return on, for example a rental property.

3. To buy a business asset you can earn from, for example a computer or stock for your business.

4. Once in a decade absolute emergencies.

Chapter 21 - Expenses

A simple financial principle is that to have more money you can do one of two things:

1. Increase your income; or
2. Reduce your expenses.

Usually in business and your personal life the easiest is to reduce your expenses.

If you want to have more money for investing, or reducing debt, or giving away, you should look at your monthly spending and see what expenses you can cut out. If you haven't done this for a long time a good rule of thumb is a 10% reduction in expenses, or 20% if you live a lavish life.

Here are some examples of ways to cut your expenses:

- Do not incur any new installment purchases.

- Do some research on your mortgage interest rate. Many people simply get a mortgage and then forget about it. Are you able to refinance at a lower rate? Do you have the option to take a lower fixed rate? Could you change banks to get a lower rate?

- Pay off any credit cards or installment plan purchases. The interest rates on these are far higher than either your home loan rate or on a personal loan from your bank. You are better off taking a new loan from your bank at a much lower rate and paying credit cards and installment debt off immediately. Of course you then have to be disciplined not to ever spend more than you have, so that you can pay your credit card bill in full every month. If this is likely to be a problem, request that your credit card provider **reduce** your limit. Or simply cut up your credit cards.

- Terminate monthly subscriptions where you are not getting great value. Gym memberships and magazine subscriptions are often money wasted.

- Eating out is usually 3-5 times more expensive than eating in. Consider this as an area for cutting your monthly expenses.

- Check your travel and entertainment budget. Do you really need to travel and have a night's accommodation for that concert or sports game?

- How much do you spend on Cable TV? Perhaps after reading the chapter on TV you can make a big saving here.

- How much do you spend on your annual vacation? Could you halve the cost and invest the difference?

- How much do you spend on coffee and snacks? Two coffees a day at $4 each is $2,920 per year! Invest that $2,920 for 20 years at 7.5% and you will have over **$135,000**!

You might be thinking that cutting some of these will curtail your current lifestyle. In the short term you are correct. But reducing your monthly expenses by 10-20% will make a huge difference over time. Too often our expenses are extravagant and frivolous. If you can cut these out and apply the money to reducing debt or making investments, in five years time you will be reaping huge dividends that will literally enable you to take your lifestyle to a whole new level.

For example if your expenses are $50,000 per year and you can cut this by 20%, you get an additional $10,000 per year. If you use this $10,000 per year to reduce debt or invest at 7.5% p.a. in five years you will have over $60,000 in additional funds. Over a 20 year period it would be over **$460,000**. You can see how simply cutting your expenses can radically improve your lifestyle over time.

Once again it comes down to living within your means and not having a lifestyle your wallet cannot keep up with.

Action Step 4:

Systematically examine your monthly expenses. Go through your bank statements and credit card bills. Try to cut your expenses by 20%.

Common Traps

Advertisers tell us to buy the latest, the biggest and the fastest. We have to resist the urge to "keep up with the Joneses". Homeowners are often guilty of this. Some people buy bigger and bigger houses in better locations and therefore increase the size of their mortgages. This increases financial stress and requires people to work harder or longer. Sometimes, this forces both parents in a family to work even when they don't want to.

Another trap is using the equity in your house to buy bigger cars or toys such as boats. Once again you are buying depreciating assets and paying interest on the additional borrowings. This can add to financial stress and the extra interest payments drain your cash-flow.

But if you are prudent there will come a time when you have so much home equity and a large disposable income that these luxuries are affordable and don't put financial stress on you.

My advice is:

1. Never rely on overtime/bonuses/commissions to fund interest payments on luxury purchases. When hard times hit the economy you will be left high and dry.

2. Ensure you do an accurate budget before buying luxury items. You must have a lot of spare disposable income.

3. Don't buy expensive toys "on the house" unless the equity in your house is more than $500,000. You might be able to afford it now, but if things get tight or a recession hits you don't want to have to sell a $50,000 boat at fire-sale prices when no-one is buying.

Chapter 22 - Five Ways to Waste Your Day

Everything you own now will either be rust or dust or be owned by someone else in 100 years time.

Critical Principle 5: **Everything you own now will either be rust or dust or be owned by someone else in 100 years time.**

Think about that! Therefore you don't actually "own" anything; in effect you are leasing it. The one thing you do actually "own" is your time. Time is the most precious commodity you have. Unfortunately it is a diminishing resource so you must use it wisely.

How you spend your day is your business. But you don't want to get to the end of your life and look back on thousands of wasted hours.

The worst ways you can waste time in your day:

1. Not Planning It

If you don't think ahead you can find yourself with an hour to spare and nothing worthwhile to fill it with. By default you might end up window-shopping, channel-flicking or dozing. Always have a plan for your day and a list of things to achieve. If you know you might have to wait for a bus or an appointment, take a good book with you. If you know you will have an hour in town between appointments make a list of the people you need to buy birthday or Christmas presents for. If you know that in any given week you have a couple of evenings free, decide ahead of time that you are going to start on a project or finish something on the house.

2. By Letting Other People Waste Your Day

Are you doing things that other people should be doing? If so they are stealing your time. Are people wasting your time with long phone calls, unproductive meetings, being late for appointments? They are stealing your time. Are your friends or partner asking you to join them in unproductive activities? They are stealing your time. You need to make a conscious decision to stop letting other people take away your most precious resource. Practice saying "No" and claim back your day.

3. By poor use of "Stress Relief" or "Leisure Time"

Yes we all need these times, and they are an important part of re-charging ourselves, but some activities are energy-sapping and some take much longer than we need. If you need to take half an hour to chill out, read a good book not a trashy magazine. Learn to play the guitar or piano rather than TV channel surfing. Listen to some great music rather than playing a computer game. Also if what you really need is half an hour of down-time, don't start watching a two-hour movie! Sure good movies are great but plan what you want to do rather than just falling into it and finding you have just lost another evening, never to be seen again!

4. By watching more than a couple of hours of TV a week – see the chapter on TV.

5. By sleeping more than you need to.

Most people need an average of eight hours sleep a night. But some people sleep a lot more than they need to. Did you know that if you spend an extra hour in bed every night you lose 23 days a year!

Let me show you what I mean:

One hour a night x 365 days a year = 365 hours.

365 hours divided by 16 awake hours per day = 22.8 days!

If you sleep more than eight hours a night and don't have enough time in your life, you have just found a solution.

Chapter 23 - Five Ways to Waste Your Business Day

Imagine if you could save four hours a week which you could devote to your job. An extra 10% effort and achievement will have a huge impact on your efficiency and your worth to an employer. Below are five common ways you can waste valuable time during your business day.

If you work for someone else, you are doing yourself and your employer a disservice. It might help your motivation if you consider that it is stealing from your employer if you engage in these activities during work time – that is exactly what it is!

If you work for yourself it is complete madness to spend time on these activities.

1. Long phone conversations

Almost all business calls can be concluded within two minutes. Just four fifteen minute phone calls take a precious hour out of your work day.

2. Joke emails

These are a complete time-waster and often a virus threat. I used to get loads of these from friends who clearly had nothing better to do. You can easily waste 15 minutes a day just clearing these emails let alone reading them, replying and forwarding them so you can waste other people's work time.

3. Surfing the internet

The amount of time you can waste on the internet is boundless. Apart from news, sport, gossip and shopping we now have social media sites. Then add music downloads, chat rooms and worst of all pornography, and you have a massive time-waster at your fingertips. Of course there are positive reasons to surf these sites (with the exception of porn) but not during work hours. Even outside work hours, you should be careful with your time and energy on these.

4. Internet Auctions

Checking and making bids on auction sites such as EBay can be a huge time-taker. This is especially the case if you are bidding on a "hot" item which you want to monitor for the last 15 minutes of an auction. Essentially your work productivity during those 15 minutes is zero. I have two suggestions; first don't bid during work hours, second if an auction closes during work hours, put in an auto-bid up to the price you are happy to pay and forget it. Incidentally this is the best auction technique in any case. If the auction goes higher than your price you are better not to participate!

5. Meetings

One of the joys of being self-employed is not having meetings. These are without a doubt the least productive, most energy-sapping time wasters of the modern corporate world. If you organize long meetings – stop! If you are required to attend – complain! In my experience emails and phone calls can resolve most decision making. If required, a meeting of the key three or four people for 15 minutes should be enough to resolve any issues. There might be two or three exceptions a year such as an AGM, but make them exceptions rather than the rule. Let me put it another way. Calculate the cost of a meeting of 20 people for three hours. That's 60 hours of people-time, plus preparation time plus loss of productivity after the meeting because everyone is de-energized and half have headaches. Let's say 80 people-hours at an average of $30 per hour. That's a cost of $2,400 which is equivalent to two extra employees that week – just from one meeting!

Here's a simple equation where T = time and W = wasting.

$$T = \$$$

$$W \times T = W\$$$

Chapter 24 - Television

One of the biggest time-wasters and therefore one of the biggest reasons why people don't spend time on setting goals and achieving them is television.

According to the A.C. Nielsen Co., Americans watch an average of more than four hours of TV each day. That works out to be 28 hours per week, or two months of nonstop TV-watching per year. In an 80 year life, the average person will have spent **11 years** glued to the tube.

Ask yourself these questions:

- How many hours a week do I spend just channel-flicking?

- How many hours of TV advertising do I see in a week (around 15 minutes per hour)?

- How many times do I go to bed later than I would like to because I kept watching TV?

- How many TV programs do I watch just because they happen to be on, not because I planned to watch them?

- In all the TV I watched last week, how did it meet any of my Lifestyle goals?

One of the best decisions our family made was to disconnect our TV from the aerial and take it out of our living room. We have a DVD player so if we want to watch a movie or a music DVD or a motivational DVD we can. Similarly, our kids do not watch TV, they watch videos and DVDs we have approved. These tend to be wildlife programs or good quality kids movies. The result of this simple change has meant we have a lot more family time, none of us waste time watching TV, our evenings don't revolve around watching a particular program at a particular time, my wife and I read a lot more, our kids are not exposed to advertisements and questionable programs (including news items on murder, rape and graphic war/terrorism carnage).

TV used to be cutting-edge technology, but that was 20 years ago. It is now an inefficient way to get entertainment and news.

Let's take news for example. I used to feel that I needed to watch the TV news most days. But let's look at it. You watch an hour of news, which is 15 minutes of advertisements and realistically you are only interested in maybe one third of the news items. The rest you just have to sit through. What you have to sit through is often so distressing and depressing (generally crime and violence and death) that you often feel violated or depressed yourself. It is far more efficient to read selected news items on the Internet or in a newspaper. Don't just take my word for it, try it for a week. Force yourself to watch no news on TV for a week – you won't miss it!

What about your favorite programs? Hey I love some TV programs. Favorites are "The Simpsons", "Friends", and "The Apprentice". So here is what I do, I buy the series on DVD! I can order any series from Amazon. Then I can watch exactly when I feel like it with no ads! Also, I can watch half a program or three programs – suddenly I'm in control. Now I am the TV program director!

If you absolutely have to have your TV plugged in, record the program you want to watch, then watch it later and fast-forward through the ads, and/or the news items you don't need to see.

Of course there are a few must-see live events such as the Olympics for example. But there are probably only 5-10 must see live events per year. It is easy to work around these, see them at a friend's place, go to a bar, get the aerial down from where you have hidden it – whatever. The point is you can live just fine without a TV, in fact I guarantee your life will be more productive and you will more easily create your Perfect Lifestyle if you don't have one.

If you have found yourself agreeing with most of this chapter, act right now! Get up and disconnect your TV or take it to a friend's place to look after it for you. I urge you to at least try it for one month – you won't regret it!

Chapter 25 - Continual Self Improvement

Continual self improvement is what life is all about. If you are not growing, you are dying. This is a universal principle that applies to every living organism. It is the reason many successful people still feel dissatisfied. You cannot stop and bask in your past achievements, you always have to grow.

Critical Principle 6:   **If you are not growing, you are dying.**

We have never "made it" or achieved all of our goals. We must always strive to be better human beings – achieving more at a higher level, and contributing more to make the world a better place. One of the best ways to continually improve yourself is to surround yourself with people who have already achieved what you want to achieve. Of course you can't always have direct access to these people, but you can usually access their story, their books, and often their course material.

I used to shun motivational books, seminars, MP3s, DVD, online videos and CDs. I think it was partly pride and partly stubborn independence. But, since I've taken time out to listen to what knowledgeable and motivating people have to say, I have gained a huge amount of knowledge and a lot of good tips. Without doubt the cost of every book, seminar and CD has been paid back to me 100 times over by the things I have learned. Sometimes you only pick up one or two new ideas or tips. But this new knowledge can unlock doors of huge opportunity.

First of course you have to make time to read books, attend seminars or listen to motivational CDs. Then you have to give yourself time to think about what you have learned and put it into action. One of my goals is to read one motivational book every week. A motivational book is any book that can inspire you to get closer to the lifestyle you want. I especially like autobiographies of successful people. They make you feel that you can be successful too. I also like books on subjects I am passionate about.

Seminars can be similar although they are usually more about acquiring knowledge. The same goes for DVDs and CDs. They can be hugely motivating.

Find books, seminars and CDs by successful people in areas you are passionate about. You will never regret the time you spend on them. You will generally find you become more focussed and more enthusiastic about the things you are aiming for.

There are hundreds of great motivational books, audios, DVD etc. Go to Amazon and start browsing!

Seminars are great for motivation and ideas. However, you have to be careful. For example, many seminars on property investment are just platforms for the organizers to sell you their properties or their software or whatever. Avoid these like the plague. The best seminars are by internationally renowned and successful speakers. They usually cost quite a lot but it is money worth spending.

Chapter 26 - World Travel

There are few activities that are as life-changing as world travel, and I don't mean going to the nearest Western country. The most mind-broadening travel in my experience is to developing countries and to cultures that are vastly different to our own. There is no way you can appreciate how incredibly fortunate and blessed we are until you have experienced other countries and cultures.

There is something outrageously mind bending about sitting in the home of a Hindu man in rural India listening to him talk about how his whole family is working seven days a week so they can afford the dowry for the arranged marriages of his two daughters because he wants them to marry an engineer or a doctor, and the dowry (unlawful but practiced everywhere) will be US$50,000 for each daughter. Then you think about the fact that there are over one billion people living in India and you begin to wonder whether our way of doing things which is so vastly different, is the right or the best way.

And there is something frightening about being in Mexico, in the border city of Tijuana and meeting people from Central America who are so desperate to get to the USA they will pay a fortune to a people smuggler, and risk the river and the guns to get there in the middle of the night. And then you wake up in the middle of the night and hear the sound of gunfire from the border.

The more you travel the more you realize we are in the most fortunate 1% of the world's population.

My advice is to travel as early in life as you can. If you can get a school or university exchange – go for it. If not, take a gap year and travel. If you are older, go overseas between jobs. I travelled alone to England when I was 16, and soon after I turned 17 I hitchhiked around Europe. I did this instead of doing an extra year at high school. I learned far more in that year than all of my friends who stayed at school put together.

You should definitely travel before you have kids. Of course it is possible to travel with kids but not on the bones of your butt, and not in flea-bitten developing world accommodation (which I recommend).

Wherever you are, whatever you are doing, whatever age you are: if you have not travelled to challenging parts of the world and seen other cultures first hand, make it a priority.

Chapter 27 - Read Widely

No matter what age and stage you are at, if you want to improve your lifestyle you should read widely and read often. This may mean disconnecting your television (see the TV chapter). But it will be one of the best things you do.

Warren Buffett (the world's most successful investor) recommends reading material completely outside your areas of interest and area of knowledge. I agree with him. I once went to the library and deliberately took out five fiction books whose authors' last name started with K. All but one were written by Eastern Europeans and they had a fascinating perspective I had never encountered before.

Fiction is often the richest source of unfettered creativity and new ideas. I spend most of my teens devouring fiction and I still read a lot today.

Of course reading the local and national newspapers is a good source of interest and inspiration. After all a newspaper is made up of dozens of small articles written by different journalists, editors, commentators, all with different ideas and opinions. I also recommend reading international newspapers. The internet is great for this. Also, most large bookstores generally carry a number of major international newspapers. It is critical to get a different perspective on the world than just our local one!

Finally of course, you should always read in your areas of passion and interest.

Buying a book is a great and cheap investment, so never hold back! And if you are having trouble locating a good book go to Amazon. Their range is global and almost exhaustive and their delivery service is impeccable, especially Ebooks which you can download and be reading within minutes.

Chapter 28 - University and Critical Thinking

I was very fortunate in that I first went to university in the 1980s. Back then my fees were $109 a year, and the student allowance was generous. This meant that I could easily afford to do a degree just for the pure pleasure of it. Hence I had a wonderful three years on campus, talking to people, writing poetry, playing my guitar, playing chess for hours with strangers in the café, and spending sunny hours with my girlfriend.

On one occasion I hitchhiked 100 miles (160 kilometers) for a Dire Straits concert. I hitchhiked back in the middle of the night. The next day I had an exam, so I slept on a bench seat outside the exam room, and my classmates woke me up before it started. My study timetable was to play my guitar up until the last possible moment and then quickly write up an essay and hand it in.

During those three years I got an A+ in Café 101 (i.e. I hung out at the café a lot), made lots of friends, got pretty good on the guitar, had a couple of poems published and thought, discussed and argued how to solve the world's problems. Now that is how university should be. At the end of three years, as a bonus, the university awarded me a BA in Psychology!

I am convinced that charging students fees for study is a policy disaster that all Western country will pay for in future generations. People should be encouraged to study and learn and think. In the current environment the commercial subjects earn a lot of money for universities and these earnings subsidise the arts and other non-commercial subjects. This of course encourages funding towards Commerce and away from the Arts. This is an unfortunate imbalance because both are important for society.

The most valuable skill I learned during my Psychology degree was critical thinking. The ability to think clearly and objectively about any information presented to me. I never got this at school, and I can't imagine my life if I had not learned this skill at an early age. I later did a Commerce degree which was (a) not nearly as interesting and (b) concentrated on learning facts, figures and methodologies, not critical thinking.

If you are just starting out in life, you should definitely go to university. The experience alone is worthwhile. But I recommend you do at least the introductory papers in Psychology, Sociology, Philosophy and perhaps History, Anthropology, Art History and a Literature paper. If you are older and busier, do a correspondence paper or go through an extramural program. At the very least go to a second hand bookshop and buy a first year text book on the subject and read it from cover to cover!

Side Note: I still come across people who think that they are not "bright" enough for university or feel that because no one from their family or neighbourhood went to university they shouldn't. For one, you don't have to be "bright" (hang around in a university café for an hour or two and you'll see what I mean) you just have to apply yourself. I would wager that 95% of school leavers would succeed at university if they took subjects they liked and put their mind to their studies.

Take "mature" students as an example. I know many people who failed at school and then in their thirties went to university and did spectacularly well. On average, mature students achieve greater success than school leavers, which I suspect is due mainly to focus and discipline. Secondly, the point of a university (as the name suggests) is that it is universally open to all. Forget what your family or friends or neighbours do or don't do.

Chapter 29 - Integrity

You will be presented with lots of "short cuts" in life. Opportunities to "bend the rules" will present themselves. You will have times where you will definitely gain an advantage by being dishonest. Sometimes lying will be the least painful option. There will be occasions when it is easy to do something you know is wrong.

But the standards you must measure yourself by are the highest levels of integrity. In fact, you cannot measure yourself by the behavior of those around you. You must measure yourself against the best you can possibly be.

By integrity I mean always acting honestly, morally and ethically.

There are three reasons why you should always act with complete integrity:

1. YOU Feel Better

Most of the time, the only person who knows if you are dishonest, immoral or unethical, is you. But letting yourself down stays with you, weighs on you and creates baggage you carry around with you. You immediately have a lower opinion of yourself which stays with you. The cost of the psychological baggage is actually much higher than the gain you accrued by your lack of integrity.

2. When Others Know

Of course many times other people are involved or observe. As soon as this happens your reputation and your trustworthiness start going downhill. There is an old saying that it takes years to build a reputation and a day to lose it.

As soon as one or two people know you are not honest or trustworthy, word spreads.

3. Some People Just Know

Even if your lack of integrity is a closely guarded secret, intuitive people just know.

Have you ever met someone for the first time and thought "They seem dishonest" or "They just don't seem right". We all have. Sometimes you just know.

The same thing will happen to you. Other people will just know you are not quite 100% to be trusted.

Practical Tests

I have two practical tests I use when I am considering doing something:

1. Court of Law

If I had to honestly describe what I am about to do in front of a judge in a court of law, would I be perfectly happy in explaining myself and answering all of the judge's questions?

If not, I simply cannot do it.

2. The Newspaper Test

If what I am about to do was reported in a balanced way in the newspaper and all my friends and family read about it, would I be happy and comfortable?

If not, then I cannot do it.

If everyone used these to simple tests to monitor their behavior, the world would be a vastly better place to live and our law courts would have nothing to do.

What is the Price of Your Word?

Some years ago it occurred to me that many people are actually willing to put a price on their word. Let me explain.

Let's say you look at a car for sale for $5,000. You tell the owner "Yes I will buy your car for $5,000. I will come and pay you tomorrow." That night a friend calls and offers you their car for $3,500. You decide to break your word and buy your friend's car.

You know what? Your word is only worth $1,500. That is the price of your honesty and integrity.

What about agreeing to lease an apartment for a year and leaving after three months?

What about promising to reimburse someone and not doing it?

What about making a pledge to charity and not honoring it?

If someone short changes me in an agreement or goes back on their word, I think:

"It must be a sad day for you today. You found out the actual price of your word and it wasn't much."

This might surprise you, but I value my word at infinity. There is no price that is high enough for me to break my word.

Let's say I decided to buy an apartment overlooking Central Park in New York for $5 million, and I had shaken hands on a deal with the owner. If an hour later I got a call from the owner of an identical next door apartment offering to sell it to me for $4 million, I would politely say no. I made a deal, my word is my bond. You cannot buy my word for $1 million, not even $1 billion, not even $1 trillion. It is not for sale at any price – ever!

In business and in your personal life you have a fantastically valuable asset – your personal integrity. **No-one** can decrease the value of this asset – except you.

Make sure your integrity and your word is never for sale – at any price.

Chapter 30 - You Only Have One Chance to be You

"It is better to fail in originality than to succeed in imitation."
Herman Melville

"Today you are you! That is truer than true! There is no one alive who is you-er than you!"
Dr. Seuss

Isn't it amazing that with six billion people on the planet, no-one has the same fingerprints as you. No-one has the same brain-print either. You have a completely unique character. I have a strong personal belief that God has given every person on earth a unique portion of His character. This means there is something in God's grand design that only you can complete the way it was supposed to be. My theory makes sense if you believe we are all created in God's image.

Regardless of your personal theology it is certain there is only one unique "**YOU**" in the world. By definition this means you can make the world a little brighter, a little more joyful and a little more like heaven on earth, in a way that no-one else on earth can!

Therefore you must be true to your inner core. You must live the real essence of who you are. You cannot and must not conform to the patterns and norms of the society you were socialized into, if they conflict with or constrain the real you.

We all know too many people who conform to what their parents want, or what their peers suggest or what society considers normal. But as we all know, the great strides in human achievement whether in art, science, architecture, technology or exploration, all required breaking out of the normal ways of behaving.

Not only that, in the final chapter of this book I discuss why one of the biggest regrets of people at the end of their life is that they were not true to themselves and too often went along with what other people expected of them.

One of the best summaries I have read on this subject is from Paul Getty's book "How to be Rich". The following is a quote from that book. Bear in mind the book was written in the early 1960s and contains stereotypes of the time. Also it was written to an audience of business executives. But look past those details because this is an excellent critique of anyone who is not living a life true to themselves:

"To be sure, there are many other pressures that force the young man of today to be a conformist. He is bombarded from all sides by arguments that he must tailor himself, literally and figuratively, to fit the clean-cut image, which means that he must be just like everyone else. He does not understand that the arguments are those of the almost-weres and never-will-bes who want him as company to share the misery of their frustrations and failures. Heaven help the man who dares to be different in thought or action. Any deviation from the mediocre norm, he is told, will brand him a Bohemian or a Bolshevik, a crank or a crackpot - a man who is unpredictable and thus unreliable.

This of course is sheer nonsense. Any man who allows his individuality to assert itself constructively will soon rise to the top. He will be the man who is most likely to succeed. But the brainwashing continues throughout many a man's career.

Consequently, the full-flowering conformist organization man takes the 8.36 train every weekday morning and hopes that in a few years he'll be moved far enough up the ladder so that he can ride the 9.03 with the middle-bracket executives. The businessman conformist is the Caspar Milquetoast of the present era. His future is not very bright. His conformist's rut will grow even deeper until, at last, it becomes the grave for the hopes, ambitions and chances he might have once had for achieving wealth and success. The confirmed organization man spends his business career bogged down in a morass of procedural rules, multi-copy memoranda and endless committee meetings in which he and the men who are his carbon copies come up with hackneyed answers to whatever problems are placed before them. He worries and frets about things that are trivial and superficial - even unto wearing what someone tells him is the "proper" garb for an executive in his salary bracket and to buying his split-level house in what some canny realtor convinces him is an "executives' subdivision."

Such a man defeats his own purpose. He remains a second-string player on what he somewhat sophomorically likes to call "the team," instead of becoming the captain or star player. He misses the limitless opportunities which today present themselves to the imaginative individualist. But he really doesn't care. "I want security," he declares. "I want to know that my job is safe and that I'll get my regular raises in salary, vacations with pay and a good pension when I retire." This, unhappily, seems to sum up too many young men's ambitions. It is a confession of weakness and cowardice. There is a dearth of young executives who are willing to stick their necks out, to assert themselves and fight for what they think is right and best even if they have to pound on the corporation president's desk to make their point.

The men who will make their marks in commerce, industry and finance are the ones with freewheeling imaginations and strong, highly individualistic personalities. Such men may not care whether their hair is crew cut or in a pompadour, and they may prefer chess to golf - but they will see and seize the opportunities around them. Their minds unfettered by the stultifying mystiques or organization-man conformity, they will be the ones to devise new concepts by means of which production and sales may be increased. They will develop new products and cut costs - to increase profits and build their own fortunes. These economic free-thinkers are the individuals who create new business and revitalize and expand old ones. They rely on their own judgment rather than on surveys, studies and committee meetings. They refer to no manuals of procedural rules, for they know that every business situation is different from the next and that no thousand volumes could ever contain enough rules to cover all contingencies.

The nonconformist - the leader and originator - has an excellent chance to make his fortune in the business world. He can wear a green toga instead of a gray-flannel suit, drink yak's milk rather than martinis, drive a Kibitka instead of a Cadillac and vote the straight Vegetarian Ticket and none of it will make the slightest difference. Ability and achievement are bona fides no one dares question, no matter how unconventional the man who presents them."

You owe it to yourself, those around you, and the world itself to be the real "**you**". It is only by being who you were created to be that you can find fulfilment and contentment.

Warning! Just because you are successful does not mean you are living the real you and doing what you were specifically designed for. Success is not necessarily a good indicator that you are living to your potential.

Let's say your specific design or calling is to organize food and shelter for the poor and needy in developing countries. You have the perseverance, tenacity, and organizational ability to do the job you were called to. But instead you shut out your call and settle for a job in a Western country where you can fully utilise all of those skills and you are well paid for them. You might be tremendously successful and rise to the top in your field. But you will be dissatisfied because you are not living your true calling, you are not being the true you.

This is why a lot of people become workaholics, or continually have something going on at every moment of their lives. We probably all know people who cannot stand an hour or two of contemplation or quiet let alone a day or a week of it. Some (not all) of these people know deep down they are not living their true calling. They need to shut out that call because they think if they heed it, their heart will become uncomfortable (true), their life will need to be changed (true), and the change will give them less of a life than they have now (**completely untrue**).

No matter how successful you are, no matter what your status, if you are not doing what your inner heart truly leads you to, you will not find true satisfaction and fulfilment in life. If you are in this situation, remember back to your teenage years and your young adult years. Think about what your dreams and aspirations were then. It is often more clear during those years. If you are currently in those years (i.e. a young adult) don't let comfort, money, or status lead you into an area that is not your true calling or your true you.

Chapter 31 - Live to Serve

Learning to serve others is difficult for most of us, perhaps especially men. We are often taught to be independent, to go out and get what we want for ourselves.

But serving others seems to be a law of nature that confers huge benefits on the person doing the serving!

Consider our modern free enterprise system. The individuals and companies that serve the most people with goods and services which have the best mix of affordability, quality and delivery are the most successful. You can apply this principle to any free-enterprise organization on earth.

What do these successful companies have in common?

- Amazon
- Fed Ex
- Apple
- Wal Mart

They are among the best at providing affordability and quality and delivering it to (i.e. serving) their customers.

In Mark 10 v 43-44 Jesus makes it a clear principle of leadership and greatness:

"Whoever wants to become great among you must be your servant and whoever wants to be first must be slave of all."

Why is it that nurses and fire-fighters are the most respected occupations? Because they serve others.

It is so easy to get caught up in our busy and sometimes selfish bubble and forget to serve others. Paradoxically this is actually much less likely to get us where we really want to be i.e. in balance, in peace, experiencing joy and fulfilment.

I can tell you in my own experience, I was not originally wired to serve. I am independent and sometimes self absorbed and often my goals are just that - "my" goals! However I have learned there are wonderful benefits to serving others. Of course I stick to what I am good at, so I don't volunteer to do flower arrangements at weddings. But I do volunteer my time and my services regularly.

These are the areas I volunteer my time:

- I mentor young people and new traders.
- I teach three half hour classes of Bible in Schools at a local elementary school.
- I run the national office and I'm on the national and international board of a mission and outreach organization.
- I'm on the board of a local youth centre, and I do the accounting and tax for them.

The funny thing is I get more out of it in terms of personal satisfaction, than I put into it. Not only that, there are studied and verified benefits of volunteering. The US government organization Americorps found that volunteers live longer, have lower rates of depression and lower incidence of heart disease. Further a longitudinal study found that people over 70 who volunteered for around 100 hours had less of a decline in health and general functioning levels than others who did not volunteer.

Prominent researcher Dr Stephen Port had this to say:

"There is now a convergence of research leading to the conclusion that helping others makes people happier and healthier. So the word is out - it is good to be good. Science increasingly says so."

Research also shows that young people who are volunteers are more likely to go on to have higher paying and higher status jobs.

Action Step 5:

If you do not already volunteer and serve others, find a way you can use your skills and abilities to help someone else.

Believe it or not it will benefit you more than them.

Chapter 32 - Little Acts of Kindness

No matter what stage our life is in, no matter how busy or stretched we are, there is always something small we can do for someone else.

These are the Little Acts of Kindness that make the world a better place to live. There are opportunities for these acts multiple times a week without even looking for them. It is up to us to be aware and be willing to see the opportunities. The powerful thing about these little acts is that most of the time we are the only person to whom the opportunity is presented. If we don't do it right then in the moment, no-one else will.

Let me give you some recent examples of little things I have done:

It was a hot day and my neighbor across the road and his brother were working outside on their new house. I took over two big ice-creams. They were delighted and we chatted about the new house.

I was taking my daughter to her school camp, and as I drove along a country road I saw a woman looking tired, hot and downcast, walking the other way. It was miles to the nearest town so I did a U-turn and asked if she needed a ride anywhere. Her car had broken down, her kids were being difficult and her ex-partner was making life hard for her. I listened to all this while I drove her to where she needed to go.

A friend of mine was going through a stressful time and had a lot going on in his life. Cooking a meal is not one of my strengths, so I put some cash in an envelope with a note to say it was for him to buy his family dinner.

I have friends who are incredibly hard working mission workers. On their return from eight months overseas, I sent them a $100 gift hamper.

A small team of us agreed to do a full day makeover of a family's house and garden. It was great fun, and I was on a high for days afterwards.

Now these Little Acts of Kindness hardly took any of my time. The money was excess to my needs. And these small gestures didn't change the world or change anyone's life. But incrementally they made the world a better place.

There are opportunities everywhere. It is our responsibility to simply keep our radars on, and our eyes open. And then be willing to take a small step out of our schedule and spend five minutes or a few dollars.

Imagine if we all did that!

Graduation

Once you have mastered Little Acts of Kindness, I suggest you graduate to Big Acts of Kindness. These take more time and more money, but they have a bigger impact. Start small, and just keep getting bigger!

Chapter 33 - You Must Have a "Purpose" and a "Why"

"I submit to you that if a man hasn't discovered something that he will die for, he isn't fit to live."
Martin Luther King, Jr.

"There is one quality which one must possess to win, and that is definiteness of purpose, the knowledge of what one wants, and a burning desire to possess it."
Napoleon Hill

If you really want to achieve something in your life you have to have a "purpose" and a "why". If you don't have a purpose to your life you won't have what it takes to tackle the obstacles life puts in your way.

You need to know why you are doing what you are doing. When you know why, you have reserves of energy and passion others don't have.

Every person who has achieved great things had a purpose and a why. Mother Teresa's purpose was to show the love of Jesus to the poor. Martin Luther King's purpose was to challenge racism and fight for civil rights. Nelson Mandela's purpose was to stop apartheid, show forgiveness and set an example for humility.

You may not have realized your purpose yet, but you need to find it.

To a certain extent you can choose your purpose. But if you really want to achieve something significant with your life, make sure the purpose you choose is one that is worthy of your life-time devotion. If your purpose is to have the best garden in your street, or to get rich or build the coolest hotrod, you might achieve your aim, but waste your potential. You might aim even higher and still miss your purpose in life.

It is my personal belief that every person has a purpose for being on earth, and that purpose involves having a lasting impact in making the world a better place. It is often easier and more comfortable to ignore your primary purpose and settle for a secondary purpose. Mother Teresa was a school teacher. She could have stayed as a school teacher her whole life and done a great job. But this was not her primary focus and she would have missed out and the world would be worse off if she had decided to stay being a teacher.

If you don't know what your purpose is, my advice is to think about the things in the world that really upset you or annoy you or make you mad – things you would like to see changed. Not all of those things will be your purpose but one of them might be.

For Mother Teresa it was poverty, for Martin Luther King it was injustice.

Find **your** purpose and make sure it's a purpose worth devoting your life to. When your goals and aspirations and dreams are aligned with your true Purpose, you become an unstoppable force for good in the world.

Here is something that seems incongruent. Your purpose may not lead you to a comfortable and easy life. On the surface it may not seem like it is creating your Perfect Lifestyle. Was ministering to the sick, dirty and dying on the streets of Calcutta easy and comfortable – no! But it was certainly Mother Teresa's chosen lifestyle. Was tackling the authorities and unjust laws and risking assassination easy and comfortable – no! But it was Martin Luther King's chosen lifestyle.

Their Perfect Lifestyles involved sacrifices and hardship. But because they had a higher purpose they were willing to sacrifice comfort and pleasure to achieve their dreams.

Critical Principle 7: **You need to find your true purpose in life and devote yourself to that.**

Of course living for your true purpose doesn't necessarily mean pouring all of you energy into one activity and ignoring the rest of your life. You will almost certainly have a number of purposes and focuses at any one time.

For example, I have a number of focuses and purposes. As a father of young children one of my main purposes is to be the best Dad and husband I can be. I also have to earn an income for my family.

Sometimes it seems like a juggling act, and in a way it is. But if you identify your key purposes in life and concentrate on those, you will find real contentment in life.

Action Step 6:

Clutter is the enemy of purpose. Our cluttered lives often stop us from clearly seeing our purpose. If you cannot clearly see your purpose, do the following exercise:

Set aside ten minutes in your day where you will be alone, quiet and undisturbed. Get up early in the morning if you have to.

Sit cross legged on the floor with you back to a wall. Close your eyes and start taking slow and deep breaths, breathing in through your nose and out through your mouth. Your tummy should be rising and falling while you breathe, not your chest.

Now imagine you are in an empty house except for the furniture, and you are looking out at a view of the ocean. Spend five minute right there looking out to sea. After five minutes of peacefully clearing your mind of any other distraction, ask yourself these questions:

- What is my purpose in life?
- How can I make the world a better place?
- Where would I feel the most contentment and fulfillment?

Do this with no pre-conceived ideas and just allow your heart (and God if you are a believer) to tell you the answers to these questions.

Write down whatever you feel. It might be just a snippet, or a thought or an idea, or a picture or a plan.

Important:

Right now, you need to take one step to action whatever it is that you felt or heard. You might need to make a phone call, search something online, order something, or talk to a friend. Whatever it is you must do it now while you have this moment of clarity. If you let it go the world of clutter will come rushing back in and the moment will be lost.

Chapter 34 - The Future You

The way you are now is **NOT** the way you are going to be in the future.

I want you to visualize the way you want to be and the person you want to be in the future.

Choose one of these timeframes:

- 5 years
- 10 years
- 20 years
- 30 years

Remember to include health and fitness, wealth, income, status, achievements, influence, family, friends and spirituality.

In the space provided write a few notes about the future you. Make sure it is the "dream" you with only positive, affirming images. Perhaps now is a good time to go back and review the notes you have made while reading this book. Who is the "you" of your dreams?

The "dream" you described above should be a perfect match with your personal goals for the same time period. If not, you need to either review your goals or your list above.

Assuming the two are now aligned, all of your primary focus needs to be on this "dream" you for every day and every week and every year until this state is attained. Remember this is not a selfish focus because the "dream" you is giving, loving and contributing. The dream you is confident, strong and supportive. The you of the future is going to be able to give far more to your family, friends, faith and community.

I have talked a lot in this book about how to achieve your goals. But I want to add a powerful psychological tool:

Act The Future You

This is a very simple but very powerful tool to help you get where you want to go. Simply start acting **now** the way you will act when you get there.

Examples:

- Say you want to be a senior business executive in five years.
- Say you want to be a fashion designer in three years.
- Say you want to be a youth worker in two years.
- Say you want to be a free lance photographer in three years.
- Say you want to own a large real estate franchise in ten years.

Decide who and what you want to be in the future and start modelling the behavior of people in that position now. Dress that way, talk that way, think that way, act that way – right now. Read the same books, attend the same conferences, join the same online forums etc.

This will have three powerful impacts:

First, your personal psychology will start to become what you want to become. Your mind will build the required bridges and links, and you will start noticing relevant situations and important facts that will build upon each other and lead you closer to your destination.

Second, the law of attraction will start to manifest itself by bringing the right people and information and opportunities to you.

Third, people will start noticing that you have the attitude and characteristics of the person you plan to be. This will make them treat you like the person you want to be, which will in turn build upon itself as a virtuous circle.

While there are many behaviors you can model, one of the most powerful is your appearance. After all you immediately create a first impression with your appearance. In fact you make an impression on yourself with your appearance. Whenever you look in the mirror you see you. Make sure it is the future you that you are looking at. Your haircut, your clothing, your shoes, your personal grooming, your watch, your shoes – all have a huge impact.

Action Step 7:

Make a list of the characteristics of the Future You. Start modelling as many of these characteristics as you can.

Write them here:

_____

_____

_____

_____

_____

_____

_____

_____

Chapter 35 - Overcoming Obstacles

For some reason part of the human condition is to face hurdles and obstacles. What stops us is that we often give up in the face of life's challenges.

Everyone experiences obstacles in life. A successful life always involves coming across obstacles and working out how to overcome them. In fact the more you achieve in life, the more obstacles you come across. The faster you are moving the more quickly you will meet obstacles! So expect to meet challenges, but also expect to overcome them. Remember that to succeed in life this is the psychology you must have. The reason unsuccessful people are unsuccessful is that they have allowed life's obstacles to stop them or derail them. We can all look back at times of our lives that this has happened. But that is the "you" of the past. The "YOU" of the future easily overcomes the challenges and obstacles of life.

There are no insurmountable obstacles to you achieving your dreams and your aspirations. There are hundreds of examples of people who had bigger challenges than you and I, but who achieved in wonderful ways and lived incredible lives.

Here is a simple Four Step process you can use to Overcome Obstacles in Your Life:

Step 1 – Prioritize Your Obstacles

Start with a blank piece of paper and write down all of the obstacles you are facing in your life right now.

Next prioritize them (put them in order of importance).

Once you have done this, pick the top three. These should be the three biggest obstacles you have. When you overcome these three obstacles, you will make a giant leap in improving your life and you will take a big step closer to your goals.

Step 2 – Exercise: Bite Sized

Start with three blank pieces of paper. Write each obstacle at the top of each page.

Each obstacle might look like this:

Obstacle 1: I don't like my job and my career path.

Obstacle 2: I am overweight and unfit and I lack energy.

Obstacle 3: I do not seem able to get ahead financially.

This is a time to be really honest with yourself about where you are compared to where you want to be.

Bite Sized

There is an old Indian proverb: "How do you eat an elephant? One bite at a time."

So now you need to take each obstacle and deal with it in single bite-sized piece at a time. This is important because if you break any obstacle into bite sized pieces you can deal with the challenge one piece at a time. Suddenly the obstacle itself does not look huge, it simply looks like a few bite-sized pieces each of which is manageable. In time you will easily prevail.

Example

Let's work through a simple example. Note: This is NOT for you to follow as I do not know your situation. It is simply an explanatory example.

Obstacle: **I am overweight and unfit and I lack energy.**

Break this obstacle into bite sized pieces, with each one leading you towards overcoming your obstacle:

Piece 1: Sustainably lose two pounds (one kilo) per month for six months.

Piece 2: Eat five portions of fresh fruit and vegetables per day.

Piece 3: Find an exercise buddy to work with.

Piece 4: Exercise 3 hours per week for Month 1, Exercise 4 hours per week for Month 2, Exercise 5 hours per week for Month 3; and so on.

Piece 5: Remove 30% of processed foods from my diet.

Piece 6: Remove 30% of non-natural sugars from my diet.

Piece 7: Drink 4 pints (2.5 liters) of water per day.

Piece 8: Cut my caffeine intake by at least 50%.

Piece 9: Reduce my junk food intake by at least 50%.

Piece 10:   Ensure I am in bed with the light off eight hours before I need to get up.

Now your "obstacle" that used to be the BIG "I'm overweight, I'm unfit, I have no energy" mountain is cut down into easily achievable bite-sized pieces that you can manage.

Do this exercise for each of the three obstacles you wrote down.

Step 3 – Look Up

To help you get motivation to succeed in consuming these bite-sized pieces, take time out to "Look Up".

Take your eyes off the obstacles and instead look up and ahead. Think about what your life is going to be like when you overcome these obstacles. Visualize the Lifestyle of your dreams and get energy, enthusiasm and motivation from where you are heading, not from what is going on right now.

Step 4 – Look Back

To get enthusiastic about taking on those bite-sized pieces it is useful to "Look Back".

Take time to look back and see how far you have come. Celebrate where you are now compared to where you were five years ago. Look back at previous obstacles you have conquered. Remember your past victories and allow them to give you power to smash through the next obstacle!

Summary

We all have obstacles and challenges in life. What separates successful and unsuccessful people is how they deal with the obstacles.

Expect to have obstacles, and more importantly expect to be victorious in overcoming them.

One of the best ways to overcome obstacles is to break them down into small easily digestible pieces. Then simply deal with each piece in turn until you have overcome the obstacle.

Sometimes we need extra motivation to get going and keep going. If you find yourself in this place take some time out to "Look Up" and "Look Ahead" to where you are going. Remind yourself how good life is going to be when you have overcome this obstacle.

It is also good to remind ourselves that we have overcome lots of obstacles in the past. We have come a long way already! Celebrate your past victories and use that strength and enthusiasm to give you momentum to tackle your current challenges.

Obstacles Self Talk

You might like to write out and repeat these self talk statements to help you reprogram your mind to overcome obstacles.

"I like obstacles because that is where I leave my competitors behind."

"I embrace obstacles because they cause me to learn and grow."

"I enjoy obstacles because they give me the opportunity to solve a problem and overcome a challenge."

Chapter 36 - Overcoming Fear

Everyone has aspirations and dreams they want to achieve, but many people don't follow through because of fear. There are three main fears that stop people from achieving the lifestyles they want:

1. Fear of Rejection

Take the classic example of the guy who meets a beautiful girl. He really wants to ask her out but the fear of rejection is too strong, and he misses out. Another example is writers who write stories or books, but they never submit them for publication for fear of rejection.

2. Fear of Failure

Some people have such a fear of failure they won't even start something or initiate a venture in case it fails. There are thousands of people with fantastic ideas for starting a business, but who never take the first step because of the fear of failure. Similarly, there are thousands of people who know they need a radical lifestyle change, but they fear the change will lead to failure.

3. Fear of the Unknown

There are numerous people who are working in jobs or careers they don't like but they won't make a change because of a fear of the unknown.

I am fortunate I am blessed with a personality that generally does not fear change or uncertainty. But I remember when I bought my first rental property and when I first started in business, I was nervous.

In order to create your Perfect Lifestyle you need to overcome these types of fears. Here is how you overcome your fears and make your world the way you want it:

(a) Identify Areas for Change

Specifically identify areas of your life you are not happy with and need change. Write them down.

(b) Identify Your Goal

Ask yourself where you want to be in five years. For example: with my dream partner, in a job/business I love, in my own debt free house, with a published novel.

(c) Admit Your Fears

Until you admit your fears specifically you cannot address them. Write down your fears. For example: "I fear the unknown and failure if I completely change my career path."

(d) Consequences

Concentrate on what your life will be like if you **don't** change, and emphasise how bad it will be! For example: "If I don't change I will be stuck in this dead end job until they make me redundant and then I'll be unemployable and I'll be broke, and I'll also die lonely because I haven't got the guts to date the person I like!"

The more you focus on the negatives of **not** changing, the more you will be motivated to change. One of the tools I use is I imagine myself as an 85 year old sitting in a rocking chair looking back over my life. What do I want to be looking back on? Success, prosperity, happiness, joy, fulfilment, successful marriage and family, opportunities taken and so on.

(e) Be Decisive

Don't prolong the pain! Make a decision right now i.e. today! Planning your next five years starts right now. Write that resignation letter now, phone the person you want to date right now! Whatever it is, start the process now.

If you are still having trouble making a decision go back to step (d) and tell yourself over and over how much worse your life is going to be if you stay in your rut.

Action Step 8:

Complete these steps (a) to (e) on a blank piece of paper. Take action today!

Remember some of the decisions you make will be mistakes, but that is okay. Mistakes are simply learning experiences. We need to allow ourselves to make mistakes and we need to allow ourselves to fail (see the chapter on Failure).

Chapter 37 - Stress

Until the middle of the 20th century the concept of stress was solely the realm of physical stress, for example stress on a piece of steel or stress on a concrete foundation. Now of course we have a publishing empire devoted to human psychological stress, and it is now a job-related sickness and even a medical condition.

But if you boil down all of the research and the plethora of books, stress is essentially:

Doing something you don't like, under pressure.

Think about it:

- Sitting in a traffic jam when you are hot and bothered and in a hurry.
- Working on a boring report for your boss until 3am.
- Trying to find a way to get the 22 items on your "must do" list done by 5pm.
- Interpersonal conflicts with close family and friends.

Of course not everything you do in a day is unpleasant. But stress is often caused by trying to fit into our day all of the activities we are really excited about, on top of those activities we have to do but are not excited about. This causes the pressure that leads to stress.

It is critical to remember it is not the volume of work that causes stress. If you are involved all day in an activity you love and are passionate about; even when you have to concentrate for hours, even if you do a 20 hour day, even if there are deadlines to meet, if you really love it you don't get stressed. Instead you get energized. Energy comes from inside, and you are likely to go into a peak state, not the opposite.

So what is the secret? Find something you **love** doing, and outsource everything in your life you don't love doing!

I recently read the autobiography of J Paul Getty who until the time of his death in 1976 was the wealthiest man in the world. He related stories of working all night long and on one occasion 72 hours straight. Stress was never a consideration. He loved building his business and so there was no place for stress.

My own story is similar (minus a few billion!). The times of my life where I have been highly stressed have always been where I have tried to fit into my day or week a whole list of activities, on top of a full-time job I didn't much enjoy. Even after I started working for myself, the stressful days were where I either put too much pressure on myself or I was involved in part of the business I really didn't enjoy.

But now I have found a vocation where I truly love every aspect of it. I experience mild stress perhaps three to four days a year. This is amazing considering I trade highly volatile financial markets where sometimes I risk losing thousands of dollars in a short time period. But in those times I find myself in a peak state where I focus and concentrate and I find it energizing and at times exhilarating.

There is only one really good thing about stress. It is a warning sign. In fact often it is the sign you need to change what you are doing or how you are doing it.

Can I make a suggestion? Pause before you seek or accept medication for stress. That could be like putting a band-aid on a broken leg. Perhaps there is an underlying problem that needs to be addressed. In my opinion, treating stress with anti-depressants is often putting a blanket over the real problem meaning that the real problem is hidden and cannot be effectively worked on.

Note: I am not a doctor or a psychiatrist. Consult your physician if you want to make a personal change in this area of your life.

If you are experiencing stress on a regular basis you must do something about it today. Research shows that chronic (long term) stress is linked to the following:

- Anxiety.
- Depression.
- Diabetes.
- Heart disease.
- Obesity.
- Tooth and gum disease.
- Ulcers.
- A suppressed immune system.

It must also be emphasized that there may well be factors under your control causing you stress or making a manageable situation unmanageable.

Examples include:

- Sleep deprivation (see chapter on Sleep).
- Poor diet.
- Lack of exercise.
- Nicotine.
- Caffeine.
- Health issues.
- Dissatisfaction with your lifestyle.

I want to be clear that not all stress can be eliminated, and not everyone can have an immediate lifestyle change. I have a very personal example to share with you.

My lovely wife Fleur was a full-time mom (the most noble and important job in the world) before our three children were at school. Our youngest child Christian is completely wonderful except that his mission in life is to change the world and push every boundary as hard as possible to see where the weak points are. He also only had two speeds, running as fast as he can or fast asleep. He is the most full-on kid anyone we know has ever seen. I could give you dozens of example but let me give you just two.

One, because he is an escape artist we have had to nail his bedroom window closed since he was 18 months old.

Two, when he was three and buckled up in his baby buggy, Fleur took her eyes off him for 15 seconds at the older children's school, and when she looked he was gone. Teachers and parents searched the grounds. Fleur realized the worst danger was the school swimming pool. Our boy had run out of the school gate, down the road and followed a pool administrator through what was always a locked door. When Fleur found him, the pool administrator was in the pool office and our three year old was walking down the pool steps into the pool; fully clothed and unable to swim.

But on with the stress story! Christian generally woke for the day at 4:30am and would try to get his way and push the boundaries until 8pm. Like all kids he would try every tactic, grizzling, crying, tantrums, hitting, kicking, biting his siblings, whining – you get the idea. Of course Fleur had to endure this all day long on her own while I was at work. No one except Fleur and I will ever know the unbelievable stress she experienced. It is testament to her that Christian is (a) alive and (b) a beautiful well-balanced, delightful boy and a strong little leader.

Of all the people I have seen and known in my life no-one has experienced the level of sleep deprivation and stress Fleur went through, and it lasted for over two years.

But in this case, no lifestyle change was possible. Fleur didn't want a nanny or caregiver. You can't just take a day off if you need it. So I understand that in some cases it is not possible to avoid stress. Sometimes you just have to utilize every support network possible and call upon God and your inner strength to get through.

Sadly there are millions of people in our world who live in far more stressful situations than this; people in war zones, refugees, slaves, prisoners etc. We need to remember them in our prayers, our actions and our giving.

To finish our personal story, if you met Christian now you wouldn't believe he was the same boy. He is gentle, kind, considerate, funny, joyful and beautiful. Once again this is testament to Fleur's patience and love. As an aside, had we gone to a doctor Christian would probably have been diagnosed as ADDH or ADDT and medicated. What nonsense! God has made him to be a world-changer, and I predict he will certainly change the world. What a terrible mistake that so many children are medicated for being who God created them to be.

Incidentally Fleur never went on anti-depressants either. Almost every doctor would have prescribed them to her. She could have ticked off almost all of the "depression" tick boxes. But she realized her stress was situation-specific. It wasn't a chemical imbalance in her brain. It was a very difficult time of life she simply had to get through; similar to times in everyone's lives for thousands of years! You learn and grow the most in your difficult times – you don't take anti-depressants.

Chapter 38 - More or Less

I have a really simple but powerful principle I use:

Do more of what is working and less of what is not working.

This principle applies across all areas of life. Let's look at some examples:

Losing Weight

If exercising works, but cutting down on carbohydrates doesn't work, exercise more.

Business

If your business has two products and one product outsells the other by 10 times, put your effort into the top seller. Perhaps make more products just like it.

Relationships

If your partner responds positively to words of affirmation but not gift giving, use more words of affirmation.

If your kids love it if you play with them in a certain way, but not so much in another, stay with what they love.

If certain people bring you down, stop associating with them.

It seems so simple, but many people keep doing the same thing over and over, even when it isn't working. I like Albert Einstein's view:

"Insanity: doing the same thing over and over again and expecting different results."

Time To Change

Think about an area of your life where you keep doing the same thing over and over but it is not working.

It is time to do less of that or stop it altogether and find another approach.

Think about an area of your life where what you are doing is producing excellent results. Try to find ways to do that activity more and more and also apply that activity to other areas of your life.

In Business

When you apply these principles to your business, make sure you test and measure your results so that you have an accurate analysis of how the changes you implement actually manifest in improvements. And remember:

Whatever gets measured, gets managed.

Action Step 9:

Take a blank piece of paper and write down one area of your life where you know this principle applies. Write down ways that you can do more of what is working and/or less of what is not working.

Chapter 39 - Risk and Risk Aversion

You are somewhere on the continuum between being a risk taker and being risk averse. Risk aversion is a measure of your preference for uncertainly over certainty. If you are too risk averse and conservative, you limit your ability to make decisions and therefore your ability to succeed. In my experience most people are somewhat risk averse. I have also noticed that those who take controlled risks in career, business and investments are generally the most successful.

For example, a risk averse person might prefer to stay in a low paid job than move jobs, or start their own business; even when such a change is likely to bring about increases in income, job satisfaction, status and so on.

Many people make choices based on the worst possible scenario rather than the likely probability of negative things happening. When I have a decision to make, it often helps me to imagine the worst possible scenario but I also:

1. Put that possibility into perspective; and

2. Make plans to ensure the worst possible scenario does not occur.

So for example if I decide to set up a new business the worst case scenario might be:

- It fails and I feel a bit embarrassed;
- I lose the time I spent trying to make it work;
- I lose a pre-defined amount of money;
- I have the opportunity cost of not doing something else with my time and money.

I can live with all of these consequences, so if I see a significant upside opportunity I am happy to set up a new business.

It might be useful for you to think about how risk averse you are. In the final chapter of this book, I note that one of the main regrets at the end of people's lives is they did not take a leap of faith or an opportunity when it was presented to them. If you are too risk averse this is a significant possibility.

There is a financial type of risk aversion called dollar fear. This is when the pain of losing $1 is greater than the pleasure of making $1. This fear often paralyses people when it comes to investments. They would rather put $20,000 in the bank at 3% interest than invest the money in a rental property. Over a long time, money in property increases in value faster than money in the bank, but some people fear the possibility of losing any of the money. Similarly, some people will not risk $2,000 to start a business even though the upside (money they could make) is hundreds of times more than the downside ($2,000).

One way to successfully control financial risk is to always protect the downside. It is far easier (and more profitable in the long run) if in any financial decision you protect or limit any losses. Let's say you have $5,000 to your name. If you set aside $3,000 to start a new business, that is all you can lose. Providing you do not sign any personal guarantees on loans or leases etc, and providing you limit your spending to $3,000 you cannot lose any more. Yet your business might be earning you $100,000 a year in two years time. It helps to concentrate on the potential upside and allow yourself to risk the funds you have put aside.

If you are very risk averse and this is affecting your decision-making, start small and get some confidence by taking small risks. Alternatively change your mind set by concentrating on what you are missing out on by not taking a controlled risk.

Of course risk aversion is not confined to business and finance. We all have risk thresholds for relationships, career, adventure, extreme sports, vacations, overseas travel, selling ourselves, asking others for their time and so on.

The important thing is to evaluate where your risk thresholds are and to think about whether your current risk thresholds are causing you to limit your opportunities, outcomes and experiences. If you recognize you are being held back by risk aversion I recommend taking small but deliberate steps to push out the boundaries a little bit at a time.

Also as we have discussed previously, use leverage to get yourself to take controlled risks. Imagine yourself in a rut doing the same thing over and over for years at a time. Imagine yourself in your rocking chair at 85 years old looking back in disappointment at the missed opportunities.

As you take small steps of controlled risk, you will find it gets easier and easier. You will find that any negative consequences are not nearly as bad as you had imagined. You will also find that you feel more alive, more excited and more stimulated. You will also be more interesting to other people. This of course all builds on itself as a virtuous circle until you are doing what you want to do without fear.

Chapter 40 - Failure

I want you to think about failure. I want you to think about the times you have failed. I want you to write down in the space below all of the words and images that come to mind when you think about the word "failure". If you are not making notes, think about it before you turn the page.

Your list might be similar to these common associations:

- Loser.
- Miserable.
- One bitten twice shy.
- Backward step.
- Painful.
- Rejection.
- Give up.
- Embarrassed.
- Feel foolish.
- Breakdown.
- Malfunction.
- Collapse.
- Disappointment.

Some people add:

- Get back up.
- Try again.
- Better luck next time.

Some people, but only a few people have positive associations.

It is no wonder most people have negative associations with the concept of failure. Our education systems, many organizations and many parents emphasize over and over that failure is bad. Even if a person tries their best, failure is more often than not criticized.

But the opposite is actually the case!

Innovation requires failure.

Improvement requires failure.

Invention requires failure.

Success requires failure.

Deep down we all know this. Let's look at some examples.

When a baby boy learns to walk he fails; over and over and over again. Does his baby diary say:

- "James failed again today."
- "James still not walking – what a failure."
- "James tried five times to walk today, failed every time. Why does he bother?"

No! His baby diary says (after 200 not mentioned failures) "Baby James walked today! Three steps on his own. We are so proud of him!"

Kids fail all the time. They fail in pronunciation, in spelling, in following a recipe, in riding a bike, in swimming. We all accept that their multiple failures are simply stepping stones on the road to success.

But as we get older we find that failure is less and less acceptable. I used to work for Mobil (now Exxon Mobil). They had a motto for senior management "one strike and you're out". How powerful is that for stifling innovation and invention? You make one mistake and you're out!

Did you know that statistically the people who are the best at anything have had the most failures? Let's look at an example. If you are a reasonable skier you can go from the top of a run to the bottom without falling over. But if that is all you do, you improve very slowly. If however you push yourself to go faster, turn more quickly, do slalom and try jumps you will wipe out many,

many times. It is only by trying new moves and failing that you improve. The same is true of just about any endeavour.

I will give you a personal example. Last summer our family went camping by a river with a big swimming hole and a long high rope swing. Most people swung out and dropped feet first into the river. But I was determined to do a full back flip. I failed over and over while I tried different techniques. I landed on my back, my ear (that hurt) and countless undignified big ugly splashes. But finally on the third day I mastered it. People even clapped when I did it. But it was only because I had failed again and again.

We need to reprogram our minds that failure is not only good, it is absolutely critical for our personal development.

Critical Principle 8: **Continual failure is required for personal growth and development.**

Some Personal Failures

I have failed many, many times in my life. I now completely accept failure as an acceptable price to pay for future success. But here are some of my failures:

1. My first job as a graduate after university was awful. My failure was in picking the wrong employer. Fortunately after 18 months I resigned and learned my lesson.

2. I have frequent failures in my trading (i.e. I lose money). I analyse these trade and I often learn valuable lessons.

3. When I ran my recruitment company I would work hard on a particular placement but fail to find the right candidate.

4. As I relate in the chapter "Bad Times and Challenges – Part 1" I once tried to make $1m dollars in one year in real estate and lost money instead.

5. I have entered short stories for publication and for competitions, and they have been rejected.

6. I have asked celebrities to do Lifestyle Interviews, and been turned down.

7. I tried to be a Rock Star, and failed.

8. I asked a billionaire to invest $25m in my fund, and was turned down.

9. I started an outdoor advertising business, and it was a glorious failure.

To help me I now use the term "Successful Failure". There are two important aspects to Successful Failure:

Fail Fast

The more quickly you fail the faster you will grow and develop. So don't wait around, don't put off the project or business or idea or asking that person for a date any longer. If you are going to fail, do it fast and move on.

Fail Cheaply

If you are going to fail, fail cheaply. Protect your downside and even if you do fail it won't cost much. This is not being negative, just wise. For example let's say you want to start a business. You don't buy $50,000 worth of product because you can get a 10% discount. You buy $500 worth of product and if it sells you buy more. If it doesn't sell you learn and move on, and the lessons you learned only cost you $500.

The real key to failure is that every failure is a learning experience. You think about what you did right, what you did wrong and what you can do differently next time.

One thing I love about failure is that it allows you to move on. If you stick with mediocrity and inside your comfort zone, you never get to move on and reach your potential. But when you step out and risk failure, then you can really start to succeed.

Embrace failure! Every failure is a stepping stone to success. In fact every failure is a gift from the world to you. The gift is the learning experience you gained.

Action Step 10:

Try something new in the next 24 hours, and if you fail, embrace it then move on!

To help you reprogram your mind to embrace failure, here are some of my favorite quotes on failure.

Copy your favorites and put them in a prominent place:

"I've missed more than 9,000 shots in my career, I've lost almost 300 games. Twenty six times I've been trusted to take the game winning shot and missed. I've failed over and over and over in my life. And that's why I succeed!"
Michael Jordan

"I don't believe in failure. It's not failure if you enjoyed the process."
Oprah Winfrey

"Failure is another steppingstone to greatness."
Oprah Winfrey

"Would you like me to give you a formula for... success? It's quite simple, really. Double your rate of failure. You're thinking of failure as the enemy of success. But it isn't at all... you can be discouraged by failure / or you can learn from it. So go ahead and make mistakes. Make all you can. Because, remember that's where you'll find success. On the far side."
Thomas J. Watson (founder of IBM)

"Making your mark on the world is hard. If it were easy, everybody would do it. But it's not. It takes patience, it takes commitment, and it comes with plenty of failure along the way. The real test is not whether you avoid this failure, because you won't. It's whether you let it harden or shame you into inaction, or whether you learn from it; whether you choose to persevere."
Barack Obama

"Failure is only the opportunity to begin again, only this time more wisely."
Henry Ford

"If you're not failing every now and again, it's a sign you're not doing anything very innovative."
Woody Allen

"I have not failed seven hundred times. I have not failed once. I have succeeded in proving that those seven hundred ways will not work. When I have eliminated the ways that will not work, I will find the way that will work."
Thomas Edison

"Many of life's failures are people who did not realize how close they were to success when they gave up."
Thomas Edison

"Success is not final, failure is not fatal: it is the courage to continue that counts."
Sir Winston Churchill

"Success is the ability to go from failure to failure without losing your enthusiasm."
Sir Winston Churchill

"Our greatest glory is not in never falling, but in rising every time we fall."
Confucius - Chinese philosopher.

"Failure is nature's plan to prepare you for great responsibilities."
Napoleon Hill

"If it fails, admit it frankly and try another. But above all, try something"
Franklin D. Roosevelt

"Ever tried. Ever failed. No matter. Try Again. Fail again. Fail better."
Samuel Beckett

"I am not judged by the number of times I fail, but by the number of times I succeed; and the number of times I succeed is in direct proportion to the number of times I can fail and keep on trying."
Tom Hopkins

"The men who try to do something and fail are infinitely better than those who try to do nothing and succeed."
Lloyd Jones

"Don't be afraid to fail. Don't waste energy trying to cover up failure. Learn from your failures and go on to the next challenge. It's OK to fail. If you're not failing, you're not growing."
H. Stanley Judd

"An inventor fails 999 times, and if he succeeds once, he's in. He treats his failures simply as practice shots."
Charles Franklin Kettering

"Once you agree upon the price you and your family must pay for success, it enables you to ignore the minor hurts, the opponent's pressure, and the temporary failures."
Vincent "Vince" Lombardi

"Many a man has finally succeeded only because he has failed after repeated efforts. If he had never met defeat he would never have known any great victory."
Orison Swett Marden

"To bear failure with courage is the best proof of character that anyone can give."
W. Somerset Maugham

"Yes, risk-taking is inherently failure-prone. Otherwise, it would be called sure-thing taking."
Tim McMahon

"There can be no real freedom without the freedom to fail."
Erich Fromm

"Only those who dare to fail greatly can ever achieve greatly."
James Arthur Baldwin

"Failure is the condiment that gives success its flavor."
Truman Capote

"Mistakes are merely steps up the ladder."
Paul J. Meyer

"A life spent making mistakes is not only more honorable but more useful than a life spent in doing nothing."
George Bernard Shaw

"My reputation grows with every failure."
George Bernard Shaw

"Keep in mind that our community is not composed of those who are already saints, but of those who are trying to become saints. Therefore let us be extremely patient with each other's faults and failures."
Mother Teresa

"Experience is simply the name we give our mistakes."
Oscar Wilde

"Winners lose more than losers. They win and lose more than losers, because they stay in the game."
Terry Paulson

"No man is ever whipped until he quits – in his own mind."
Napoleon Hill

"All my successes have been built on my failures."
Benjamin Disraeli

George (Babe) Ruth has many times been voted the world's greatest baseball player. He was the first player to hit 60 home runs in one season (1927), and this record stood until 1961. His lifetime total of 714 home runs was a record at his retirement in 1935 and was a record until 1974. His .342 lifetime batting is the tenth highest in baseball history, and he still holds the Yankees season record of .393 (1923). His .690 career slugging percentage and 1.164 career on-base plus slugging (OPS) are still major league records. But until 1964 **he also held the record for the most strike-outs** (1,330).

Here are three wonderful quotes from Babe Ruth:

"It's hard to beat a person who never gives up."

"Every strike brings me closer to the next home run."

"Never let the fear of striking out get in your way."

Chapter 41 - Focus

If there is one word that summarizes what it takes to be successful in life it is **Focus**.

Whatever you Focus on You Will Achieve

Whatever is Focused on gets Acted Upon

Think of anyone who has experienced outstanding success. The common theme will always be focus:

Thomas Edison
Muhammad Ali
Walt Disney
William Shakespeare
Elvis Presley
Gandhi
Frank Sinatra
David Beckham
Martin Luther King

It doesn't matter who you think about, if they have achieved exceptional success it is because they focused on their one pursuit to the exclusion of every other hobby, interest, pastime or passion.

Many successful people are so focused it borders on obsession. I am not advocating that because balance is just as important. But focus is the key to success.

I read Warren Buffett's biography recently, and there were a number of stories about his focus. For example Warren and his wife would sometimes have dinner parties at their home. On occasion, halfway through dinner, Warren would simply get up from the table, not say anything and go upstairs to his office and read annual reports. Can you imagine inviting a group of friends for dinner and disappearing to go and focus on your overriding passion?

In fact both Warren Buffett and Bill Gates are on record stating that they attribute their success to one trait: Focus.

This from Bill Gates:

*"I've learned that only through **focus** can you do world class things, no matter how capable you are."*

Bill Gates Sr. once asked Warren Buffett what was the most important thing in achieving in life? Warren Buffett answered "**Focus**".

Let me quote from Warren Buffett's biography:

"He [Warren Buffett] *ruled out paying attention to almost anything but business – art, literature, science, travel, architecture – so that he could focus on his passion."*

The principle of Focus is evident in my life and I bet it is in yours. The most success you have had in life will have been where you have focused your time and energy. Not only that, but the areas of your life that have been unsuccessful have been the ones where you have *not* focused your time and energy. In fact if you think right now about what is great in your life and what is not, you will be able to see immediately where you have focused:

- Your Relationships
- Your Career
- Your Fitness
- Your Weight
- Your Marriage
- Your Finances

So practically, what do we need to do if we really want to succeed in a specific area of our lives?

In order to have a balanced and full life there are three areas that have to take priority over your passion, or any specific focus:

Faith, Family, and Friends

These must be your Primary Focus.

Once you have made sure that these are your Primary Focus, you should give all of the rest of your focus to your Passion.

In this way you will achieve both a balanced life **and** outstanding achievement.

So to summarize:

Primary Focus

Faith, Family, Friends

Secondary Focus

Your Passion

"The successful warrior is the average man, with laser-like focus."
Bruce Lee

"Most people have no idea of the giant capacity we can immediately command when we focus all of our resources on mastering a single area of our lives."
Tony Robbins

Chapter 42 - Bad Times and Challenges Part 1

If anyone tells you there will not be bad times – run! They are either lying or ignorant. It is part of the human experience to encounter many difficult and trying times. The key therefore is how we deal with bad times when they arise.

Because it is far better from a psychological point of view to consider all bad times as challenges to overcome, for the rest of this chapter I will use the words "challenges" or "obstacles". I suggest you start using this terminology in your own life. This way, you train your mind to think that any difficulty is just a challenge to prevail over or an obstacle to get around.

I have experienced many challenges in my life. The most poignant to this book is the challenging year I had in 2006.

As you know I like to set goals. So I started on 1 January 2006 with a number of clear goals for the year. I also like to have big goals. My big financial goal was to make $1m that year. I not only had a goal, I also had a strategy – to buy, renovate and sell 20 residential properties with an average gain of $50,000.

20 x $50,000 = $1,000,000

Easy!

My total income for the previous year was under $100,000, so this was a big stretch goal.

However I had a number of factors on my side:

- I had previously renovated five properties so I knew what I was doing. I also knew how to add value rather than add cost.
- I had bought and sold a number of properties and I really did understand the residential real estate market.
- I had a loan facility that would allow me to buy and renovate, providing I turned each property over quickly.
- The property market was booming and properties were selling on average in 20 days.
- I had great group of reliable trades people to do the work.

After a good period of looking I found an excellent property with the following positive features:

- A private seller willing to sell $15,000 under market value.
- A nice house on a lovely section that would appeal to families.
- Lots of ability to improve the property at a low cost.
- A great area and sought after location.

I bought the house in February 2006 for $410,000. I borrowed the whole amount at 9.2% p.a.

The renovation took six weeks and cost $14,291, also borrowed at 9.2%.

Therefore the cost per week to hold the property was $750.

I was so pleased with the result and so confident of the market, I started to market it at $520,000 which would have given me an $85,000 gain if I sold it quickly.

I advertised the property and floods of people came through it. Everyone loved it. I had a number of comments that it was the best presented property on the market. Everyone loved it – but nobody bought it.

This happened for week upon week. I started dropping the price. As the weeks passed, the prime mid-summer selling season finished and the autumn arrived. I continued to advertise and I continued to drop the price. The flood of viewers turned to a trickle.

Around this time a few unfortunate coincidences occurred. First, my main source of income, my recruitment business went into its worst ever year. For years, I had budgeted for income of around $40,000 for the autumn quarter, the actual was $6,177 which only just covered the costs of running the business, excluding the lease. Second, I had just taken on my first full-time employee and he had to be paid. Third, a big rental property I owned suddenly became vacant and just before winter it was proving impossible to rent out. It went from $600 per week in rent to $0. The outgoings on the property were $525 per week.

Fourth, I had also employed a full time employee to build up an internet real estate company I had purchased. I budgeted for the business to at least pay his salary. It didn't even come close.

Fifth, expecting a good year we were in the process of doing a major ($150,000) renovation on our house. Much of the work had been done and now the invoices were coming in; builders, plasterers, plumbers, glazers, joiners etc.

Sixth, the booming property market turned. It didn't turn bad immediately, but the real heat and bubble went out of it. Any excess I hoped to get from the hot market evaporated. Buyers began to sense that it was no longer a sellers' market and the tide was turning.

By now, it was winter and I had a house I couldn't sell, a rental property I couldn't tenant, two full time employees to pay, my own mortgage to pay, an office lease to pay, renovation invoices to pay and a wife and three children to feed, clothe and look after.

What started on 1 January looking like being a hugely profitable year, quickly turned to a nightmare.

From April onwards my monthly outgoings (excluding paying for our own renovation) were $15,000. My total monthly income was $0.

Now I have a very good and solid and long relationship with my bank. I managed to increase my borrowings to the absolute maximum they would allow. Of course I then had to pay the interest on the additional borrowings, and I knew if the situation didn't change soon, I was in real trouble. If I had to sell my properties in mid-winter at fire sale prices, I could conceivably lose everything including my half-renovated home.

At such times as these, when you are a man of God, you pray! And you seek God. I really only wanted one thing – for God to step in and fix my problems. Did He? Well no actually. Frustrating isn't it to get the realization that we are His servants and not the other way around! For more details on my spiritual journey during this difficult time see the Bonus Chapter "Bad Times and Challenges - Part 2".

Instead I went through the somewhat humbling experience of telling the people I owed money to that I had to pay them in monthly installments. I had to tell my employees (who were friends) that the business was not performing, and I was in trouble. I had to try and stay positive and keep trying to keep everything together.

I was really into the last couple of weeks of cash, and I still had unpaid bills. Finally things started to happen. I unexpectedly sold a domain name for $5,000. Soon after, I finally got tenants for my rental property. Then with one last attempt with a big ad in the newspaper I found a buyer for the house.

In the end my $15,000 per month outgoings and zero income lasted for six months and took away $90,000.

I had to sell the house for an $11,000, loss – but I was delighted to sell it, to stop the money drain and the emotional pain!

I didn't suddenly bounce back either. It took another six to nine months to get back to feeling like everything was fully afloat again.

I had never really understood before that you really do learn the most from life's challenges. I learned more in that year about myself and money than I had in any successful year.

What is the lesson? You will have challenges and obstacles in your life. In fact the higher you aim, the larger the obstacles will be. Go into every new experience expecting challenges but with a quiet confidence that you will succeed. If you have a convergence of challenges that completely overturn your plans and your life, take a deep breath and realize that life has just given you a gift – a wonderful learning opportunity. You will emerge stronger and wiser and more humble.

Chapter 43 - Determination, Diligence and Perseverance

There are three mindsets successful people have that enable them to use every failure as a learning experience and a stepping to future success.

1. Determination

Determination simply means coming to the point of certain decision. No wavering, no maybes, but a definitive decision. For example:

- I will write a book.
- I will start a business.
- I will get a degree.
- I will be a professional golfer.
- I will become a millionaire.
- I will double my business profits next year.
- I will buy my first investment property.
- I will launch my own website.

Unfortunately many people are not good at making decisions. Even fewer people make absolute certain decisions and follow through. This is a very important mental state to get into if you want to succeed. Be decisive and be determined that nothing can stop you.

2. Diligence

Diligence is the persistent exertion of body or mind to achieve the decision you have made.

Above all, you much be persistent. Give your project high energy and give it momentum. Diligence is often used interchangeably with hard work. It means sometimes starting early and working late. It means concentrating while everyone else is slacking off. It means working to achieve your goal while everyone else is on vacation. It means doing five hours preparation when everyone else is doing one hour.

When I was studying for my honours degree, my certain decision was to achieve first class honours and get no less than A for each of the six papers I had to sit. For nearly a year my car was the first student car in the car park every morning and the last to leave. When everyone else was on Easter break, I was studying. I made sure every assignment was the best I could make it. And I achieved my goal.

I have a friend David Pierce who heads up an amazing international missionary organization www.steiger.org. God uses David in incredible ways in unbelievable places. I heard David talking once about Bible studies he did for his kids when they were in high school. There were his two boys and two or three others – so five kids for a 45 minute after school Bible study. David did six hours preparation for each of those little studies, praying, seeking God, studying! He was diligent with the task at hand, and no wonder he now has a powerful international ministry. I sometimes wonder if human beings are designed specifically so that only those who diligently persevere achieve great things.

I like what author Stephen King said:

"Talent is cheaper than table salt. What separates the talented individual from the successful one is a lot of hard work."

And what famous Basketball player Magic Johnson said:

"Talent is never enough. With few exceptions the best players are the hardest workers."

3. Perseverance

Perseverance is simply a granite-hard resolution that no matter what, you won't quit or give up or turn aside from the course you have set or the goal you are pursuing. If you set your mind that nothing will stop you – nothing will!

Sadly most people give up at this very step. You might set the right goal, have the right environment and have a sure recipe for success, but if you don't have perseverance you will not succeed. Why? Because life is designed to give us hurdles and challenges and obstacles. Not only that but the bigger the goal, the greater the challenges. I sometimes wonder whether God made the world like that on purpose so when we achieve our goals He can say "Ah so you really did mean it! Here are the blessings that come from your perseverance!"

I can't emphasize strongly enough how important this is. The great inventions, the great strides in progress, the great leaps in human understanding have been born out of perseverance.

Critical Principle 9:   **Perseverance is the mother of achievement.**

Let's look at some examples:

Walt Disney

It is reported that Walt Disney was declined by 302 banks for financing Disneyland. I have written on my wall:

"Walt Disney was turned down 302 times in persevering with his dream. How many times am I willing to be knocked back to achieve my dreams?"

"The difference in winning and losing is most often, not quitting."
Walt Disney

Soichiro Honda

Soichiro Honda applied for an engineering job with Toyota after World War Two, but was turned down. He was unemployed until his neighbors starting buying his "home-made scooters". He went on to start his own company – Honda.

Colonel Sanders

Colonel Sanders reportedly tried to sell his fried chicken recipe over 1,000 times before he found a buyer! Seven years later he sold his company for $15 million.

How many doors will you knock on?

Stephen J Cannell

Stephen Cannell was one of the most successful writers and producers in TV with shows like 21 Jump Street, The A Team, Wiseguy etc.

However he failed badly in school because he was dyslexic. Before he had sold one story, Stephen Cannell wrote for five hours a day, seven days a week for five years. That is a total of 9,100 hours of writing *before* he sold one story. No wonder he was so successful.

Imagine what you could achieve if you spent five hours a day, seven days a week for five years focussing on your one passion! The whole world could hardly contain your success!

John D Rockefeller

Adjusting for inflation, John D Rockefeller is often regarded as the richest person in history.

"I do not think there is any other quality so essential to success of any kind as the quality of perseverance. It overcomes almost everything, even nature."
John D. Rockefeller

Author "Failures"

John Grisham's first novel was rejected by 16 agents and 12 publishers.

Stephen King's first novel was rejected by dozens of publishers.

J K Rowling's first Harry Potter book was rejected by more than 10 publishers.

William Golding's classic "Lord of the Flies" was rejected by 20 publishers.

Robert M Pirsig's book "Zen and the Art of Motorcycle Maintenance" was rejected by 121 publishers. It has gone on to sell millions of copies in 27 languages.

Chicken Soup for the Soul was rejected over 130 times. Now the "Chicken Soup" series has sold more than 80 million copies.

The British mystery author John Creasey received 743 rejections from publishers before he was finally published. That is the equivalent of one rejection letter a week for over 14 years! You just know someone with that much perseverance is going to succeed. Creasey went on to publish over 600 books.

If you are writing a book, how many publishers will you go to?

J. Paul Getty spent nearly a year drilling oil wells with no success. One the verge of giving up, he tried one last time – successfully.

How many dry wells will you drill?

Decca Records rejected the Beatles saying "The Beatles have no future in show business".

Will you accept it when someone rejects you or your plans?

Summary:

You need to develop three mindsets so you can use every failure as a learning experience and a stepping to success:

- Determination.
- Diligence.
- Perseverance.

Chapter 44 - Limiting Beliefs

What stops people from achieving their full potential in life? What is it about people who fall short of the heights you would expect them to scale?

It can't be lack of education.

It can't be lack of money.

It can't be coming from a broken home.

It can't be _____ (fill in this space)

- because millions of successful people have had all of these obstacles and more in their life.

What stops most people from reaching what they are capable of is their own internal limiting beliefs about what is possible for them. Have you ever noticed that top sportspeople, business leaders, political leaders and high achievers have a quiet (and sometimes not so quiet) confidence in themselves? The opposite is true of people who do badly or are down and out. These people lack confidence and often speak negatively about themselves. In short, they have strong limiting beliefs about themselves.

The fact is all of us have limiting beliefs in some areas at some level. The problem with limiting beliefs is they disempower us and cause negative consequences. Even if you have great success in 90% of your life you might find you have a limiting belief that is holding you back in one or two areas.

You might have a great business and be fit and healthy but if you a hold the limiting belief "I am not good at relationships, I may as well stay single" you are going to experience negative consequences.

Everything might be great for you, but you hold the limiting belief "I will only ever have enough money just to get by". That is disempowering and is going to hold you back in many ways.

You might recognize some of these:

"No matter what I do I'll always be overweight."

"I'll never make progress in my career because I don't have the education."

"The best result I can get is a bit above average."

The good news is we can identify our limiting beliefs and deliberately cut them out of our minds and replace them with empowering beliefs.

The next step is a really powerful way to literally re-program your mind so you reverse your most disempowering limiting beliefs. I know it is easier to just keep reading rather than stopping to do the exercise but I really encourage you to take five minutes out because this can be powerfully effective.

Action Step 11:

Write down the three limiting beliefs that have been holding you back the most. Under each one, write down the negative consequences you have already experienced through holding each belief.

For example:

"No matter what I do I'll always be overweight."

Makes me feel hopeless. Makes me give up trying.

"The best result I can get is a bit above average."

Causes me to put up with mediocrity.

"I am no good at relationships; I may as well stay single."

Keeps me from meeting good people, one of which could be a great partner for me.

Then on a separate piece of paper write each limiting belief with a space under each one. Now write down an opposite empowering belief for each. Then most important, cross out the limiting belief.

For example:

~~"No matter what I do I'll always be overweight."~~

"I can be slim, fit and in great shape!"

~~"The best result I can get is a bit above average."~~

"I can achieve excellence if I put my mind to it!"

~~"I am no good at relationships; I may as well be single."~~

"I love people, people love me, and I'm going to be the perfect partner for someone!"

Close your eyes and see yourself actually cutting those limiting beliefs out of your mind and putting them in a blender and blending them. Then pour them into your sink and see them get washed away.

Write your three new empowering beliefs on a new piece of paper and read them aloud to yourself every day with energy and enthusiasm. I have used this technique myself, and it really works.

Chapter 45 - Mental Barriers

No matter who we are or what we do, we all have mental barriers that get in the way of what we want to achieve.

In almost all cases these mental barriers have no basis in reality. Most of the time they are barriers put up because of our upbringing, education or culture.

Consider the following statements:

- "I'm not bright enough to go to college."
- "I don't have the confidence to talk to an audience."
- "I don't have the skill to play that sport."
- "I couldn't be successful in business."
- "I will never be in that financial position."
- "I can't achieve what he has achieved."
- "That goal is beyond me."

All of these statements represent a mental barrier that is irrational and has no basis in reality. You probably have many similar statements or mental barriers you allow to get in your way. Consider the "Four Minute Mile Barrier". In the late 1940s it was considered impossible for a human being to run a mile in under four minutes. The majority of runners and the public believed this. Because the mile runners believed it, no-one ran the mile in under four minutes. This is until May 1954 Roger Bannister ran it in 3:59:4.

Interestingly only six weeks later Bannister's record was broken and after that, four minute miles were commonplace. Once the mental barrier was broken, people's performance matched the reality that a mile could be run in under four minutes.

You need to think about and analyze your own mental barriers because they are what hold you back, not the reality of what you can achieve.

Sometimes we speak out our mental barriers "Oh I could never do that" but most often we think them.

Action Step 12:

Just like Action Step 11, take a blank piece of paper and write down the three main limiting mental barriers you either speak or think.

Once you have done that, write down an opposite positive statement for each. Then most important, cross out the limiting mental barrier.

Some examples:

"I could never afford that."

"How could I afford that?"

"I often feel sick and tired."

"I'm healthy and fit and I don't get sick."

"I could never start a business."

"I would be very successful in business."

"I could never be that good."

"I excel at everything I work hard at."

"I'm not good enough to get that job."

"I am able to succeed at whatever job I do, and I would be great at that job."

Once again write down your positive statements on a piece of paper and repeat them aloud every day.

You can literally re-program or re-socialize your mind by repeating the positive statement and developing the habit of thinking and speaking positively. This effectively breaks down any limiting mental barriers.

"It's the repetition of affirmations that leads to belief.
And once that belief becomes a deep conviction, things
begin to happen."
Muhammad Ali

Chapter 46 - Words and Self Talk Part 1

One of the most important but sadly one of the most overlooked factors that affect what we can achieve is self talk.

Researchers have found that of the tens of thousands of thoughts a person has every day, a huge percentage are negative. Often we vocalize these statements and many times we don't even realize it!

Consider the following:

"What an idiot I am."
"I'm so stupid."
"I'm useless."
"I'm pathetic."
"I suck at that."

Then there is the more serious and often not vocalized negative self talk:

"I will never succeed."
"Life is passing me by."
"I will never achieve my goals."
"Nice guys finish last."
"I can never lose weight."
"I'm ugly."
"No-one likes me."

The amazing truth about self talk is you gravitate towards and become what you say to yourself.

If you say to yourself "I can never lose weight", that becomes an actual reality for you.

If you say "I will never achieve my goals" that will be true – you never will!

We often use words that are damaging to ourselves and others. We don't mean to. It is simply that very few of us have been taught just how powerful words, especially spoken words, really are.

Why is it that great orators and speech makers can move us?

Why is it that great coaches can motivate a team with words?

Why is it that great actors can change our emotional state with their words?

Why is it that words can build a child's self esteem or shatter it?

How is it that the words of a song or a book or an advertisement can change our behavior?

How is it that a well worded argument can change our opinion?

How is it we can be deeply hurt, sometimes for years, by words spoken to us?

Because words are **far** more powerful than we have been taught to believe.

Critical Principle 10: **Words are far more powerful than we have been taught to believe.**

Because of the huge power words and therefore of self talk, it is critical to pay attention to what you are saying to yourself. The good news is you can practice positive self talk and over time you can change your self talk and therefore your reality by only saying positive things.

There are three techniques I have found very useful:

1. Deliberate Positive Statements

I go for a walk and I repeat a number of positive statements to myself such as:

"I'm going to be energetic, enthusiastic, and feel great all day"

"I'm healthy and fit and I don't get sick"

"I'm going to be the best dad and husband in the world"

These statements focus me on what is important, and cause me to feel and act the way I have spoken it.

2. Override Negative Self Talk

I ensure that I eliminate any negative self talk whether thoughts or verbalizations. If I catch myself in negative self talk, I will over-ride it with a positive statement.

3. Gratitude

Speaking aloud how grateful you are is a powerful way to reinforce positive thoughts and attitudes. We all have many things we can be grateful for:

- Eyes that see.
- Ears that hear.
- A heart that beats.
- Good friends.

- Family.
- A full stomach.
- A roof over our heads.
- Our faith.

I start my daily prayer and meditation simply being grateful to God for all of the blessings of my life. It is a great way to stop my focus being on challenges I have or areas of my life I am not happy with.

I also like Jack Canfield's suggestion that we use self talk as a reverse-paranoia statement:

"Everyone is part of a global plot to enhance my well being."

That is a powerful positive self talk statement, and it is printed on my wall.

Action Step 13:

Write out ten positive and affirming self-statements and repeat them aloud five times each day. In three minutes a day you will (over time) transform your attitude, your behavior and your reality.

Have you ever met someone who was determined to achieve something? Someone whose determination propelled them past others who were more naturally gifted? Determination is simply the physical outworking of self talk statements such as "I will succeed" "I will never give up" "I'm going to make it no matter what gets in my way".

To paraphrase the philosopher Frank Outlaw:

Thoughts become Words
Words become Actions
Actions become Habits
Habits become Character
Character becomes your Destiny

Positive self talk is a key to a huge door in your life. Unlock that door and you will find significant personal development will follow.

Chapter 47 - Perfect Week

I have developed a concept I call "Perfect Week". The idea behind Perfect Week is that you sit down on a Sunday night and plan every day for the next seven days. But you not only plan it, you ensure that in every area you have control over, you do exactly the right thing. So this is not a vacation week, and it is not a daydream week where you find $100 bills and everyone is nice to you and every coincidence is favourable. Rather this is a normal week where you are disciplined to do everything you want and need to do.

I will give you a cut-down version of my Perfect Week to give you the idea.

Every Day

- Get up at 6am and go for a walk on the waterfront and pray.
- Morning Lymphasise/Prayer/Meditation
- Read the Bible
- Eat at least five portions of fresh fruit and vegetables.
- Drink at least four pints (two and a half litres) of water.
- Send one email that takes me closer to a goal.
- Write for one and a half hours.
- Pray individually with each of my kids before bed.
- Spend at least half an hour of quality time with my wife.

Specific Days

- Workout at the gym on Monday, Wednesday and Friday.

- Go for a 45 minute prayer walk on Tuesday and Thursday.
- Do at least one hour preparation for my Bible in Schools classes on Tuesdays.
- Pray with friends on Tuesday night.

Over the Week

- Read one motivational or educational book.
- Spend at least 10 hours quality time with my kids.
- Have a date night with my wife.

The interesting thing is that even though it looks achievable on paper it is extremely difficult to achieve in reality. However I thoroughly recommend you plan a Perfect Week and try as hard as possible to achieve it.

It will highlight two things:

1. How far your normal week is from your Perfect Week (i.e. great motivation to make some changes)?

2. How many incidental and unimportant things you allow to creep into your life?

When you are 85 and in your rocking chair don't you want to look back on weeks you either achieved your Perfect Week or got close? I have a feeling that many people will look back and see the mountain of distractions that caused them to live at a far less fruitful and abundant and contributing level than they would have liked.

Chapter 48 - Create Your Day

For many people the concept that you can "Create Your Day" is strange or incomprehensible. That is because for most people the events of the day just happen, and they react to whatever the day brings. But that should not be, and need not be the way you live your life.

As outlined in the chapter on self talk, we have an incredible power to speak into our lives and thereby affect the reality around us.

There are three keys to creating your day:

1. Expectation

Expect good things to happen to you today. Expect positive encounters. Expect God to bless you. Expect to have creative ideas, to be happy and cheerful and to achieve great things. Just starting your day with these expectations will change your attitude and the way you see and experience life.

2. Meditation

This has nothing (necessarily) to do with religion or your spirit. The word meditation simply means "continued or extended thought; reflection; contemplation".

If you can discipline yourself to start your day or your work day with five minutes of quiet thinking about the day ahead, you will make a huge positive impact on what happens in your day.

When I arrive at work, the first thing I do is spend at least five minutes meditating about the day ahead.

There is probably no other daily activity in the world that will give you a greater return on your time than investing this five minutes!

3. Eradication

Eradicate and do not allow negative thoughts or negative events into your day. Of course you cannot control all of the events of your day. However, in areas you do have control over, don't allow bad situations to arise. For example avoid arguments and conflicts, do not spend time with people who bring you down, read and listen to and watch things that are going to motivate you and encourage you and not bring you down.

You and no-one else owns your day. You get to choose 99% of what happens to you today. If you are in a situation that requires you to spend your day doing something that de-motivates you and brings you down – YOU must do something about it.

In areas you don't have control over, choose to look at the positives in any challenging situation. Try to turn it around to bring good out of it.

With discipline and practice we can take full control of our thoughts.

We can eradicate negative thoughts and by doing that, create a day that becomes more positive, creative, loving, effective, and therefore more life-changing.

One of the main attributes of our humanity is that we can change who we are, what we feel, what we believe and what we achieve. The start of that process is changing our thoughts and attitudes from negative ones that suck life out of us to positive ones that lift us up and recharge us.

Once you start directing your day from the start and taking control of how you think about yourself and what is happening to you, you will find you can actually shape your day and even create your day. Wouldn't that be a wonderful way to live!

Action Step 14:

Write down your five minute meditation and starting tomorrow; begin to create your own day.

Introduction To Bonus Chapters

The following six chapters are **free** Bonus Chapters.

You have not paid for these chapters; they are included as an addition to this book.

If you do not read the bonus chapters, you have still read the whole book.

Of course I hope you read them because they contain key reasons why I have True Balance in my Lifestyle.

Bonus Chapter - True Balance

In the developed world we are comfortable talking about balancing "all" the areas of our lives:

- Our work life.
- Our family life.
- Our physical health.
- Our minds.
- Our love life.

But a lot of the time we forget or are uncomfortable about exploring our spiritual life. This reticence is a strangely Western and "modern" phenomenon. In fact, studies and census data show that around 92% of people believe in the existence of a higher power. All of the world's major religions teach that God is capable and interested in interacting with us!

If so many of us believe it, why do so few of us include it in our search for a truly balanced life?

In my opinion, the reason many people do not feel fulfilled and content even after they have achieved and "balanced" their lives is that they ignore their spiritual life.

Nowhere is it more clearly stated than in John 10 v 10 where Jesus said:

*"I have come that they may have life, and that they may have it more **abundantly**."*

This is a key truth for living. All of us want to live life to the full and to live abundantly. What does abundance mean?

- Plenty
- Wealth
- Great quantity
- Loads

So practically what does this mean?

It is my belief that part of our design is to have a relationship with God. In other words, God designed us so that having a relationship with Him is an integral part of our humanity.

If I am right, it is not possible to live a balanced life without working on our spiritual life as much as we do our hearts, our minds and our bodies:

Jesus answered: "Love the Lord your God with all your heart and with all your soul and with all your mind and with all your strength."
Mark 12 v 30-31

Taken a step further, if you believe what Jesus said, we need to focus our heart, soul, mind and body on God first to find true balance.

This is made clearer in Matthew 6 v 33:

But seek first his kingdom and his righteousness, and all these things will be given to you as well.

How does this relate to creating your Perfect Lifestyle? My experience is that a Perfect Lifestyle requires perfect balance. As such it is not possible to perfect your life unless it is God-centered.

Let me be clear. It is possible to have a good life without God. It is possible to have a fun life without God. It is possible to have a great life without God.

But it is not possible to have a fully abundant life reaching the potential and level of contentment you were created to have, without a God-centered life.

In my life and having observed hundreds of others, a God-centered life gives a level of direction, vision, hope, peace, joy and fulfillment that takes you to another level.

Does this make me feel smug? Superior? Proud? Absolutely not!

Am I so certain that I am dogmatic? No.

Am I judgmental or narrow-minded in my faith? No.

I am just like everyone else on this journey called life, trying to find the perfect balance and the perfect life.

True Balance

Again, Mark 12 v 30-31:

Jesus answered: "Love the Lord your God with all your heart and with all your soul and with all your mind and with all your strength."

In the Christian sense, this is true balance; to love God with:

1. Our heart – the part of us that loves. This includes our emotions and the things we love in an emotional way.

2. Our soul – the part of us that will exist forever. This is the part of us that communicates with God and has a relationship with God. If you believe God exists and you will (in some form) exist in 1,000 years – this is the most

important part of who you are. Sadly, this is the part of us we are most likely to ignore or feel uncomfortable about.

3. Our mind – the part of us that thinks and reasons and makes decisions.

4. Our strength – our physical bodies; our actions and our movements; the things we say and do and cause to happen.

The purpose of this chapter is to emphasize the importance of complete balance, which means working on your spirit as much as you work on your body or your mind. If everything else is in balance but you still do not feel content or feel you are living life to the full, it is very likely that this is the area of your life you have been ignoring.

My Advice

If you have not worked enough on your spirit life here is my personal advice:

1. Pray

Praying is simply talking to God.

If you haven't talked to God for ages, find somewhere quiet or, go for a walk and just talk to Him!

Ask especially for wisdom, and help in re-establishing communication with Him.

Ask for good things; both for yourself and others.

Ask for Him to make His presence felt in your life.

2. Read the Bible

The Bible is God's word to us. It reveals His character and His message to humanity.

3. Listen

Make time and space in your day for God to "speak" to you – through the Bible, through books, through people or more directly through feelings or impressions in your mind.

4. Spend time with like-minded people

Find a church or group of people who share your beliefs or share your interest in searching out spiritual truth. No-one, and I mean no-one has "arrived" in their spiritual life. We are all on our own personal spiritual journey; learning and growing on the way.

5. The Cross

The story of the New Testament is simple. God and humanity have been separated by all of the wrongdoing in the world (if you don't know what I mean watch the evening news or think about the worst, most selfish thing you have ever done).

Our wrongdoing carries the death sentence.

But God sent his only son Jesus to die on the cross, in our place.

Now that Jesus has paid the price and made the ultimate sacrifice on our behalf, we simply have to acknowledge God's gift to us and start living our lives for Him.

I have to say from experience that no half-hearted measures work with God. Either you give your life fully to Him or not at all.

But remember, there is absolute truth in the universe. Your main purpose on earth is to find that truth.

You will seek me and find me when you seek me with all your heart.
Jeremiah 29 v 13

Relationship With God

If you who don't know how to begin a relationship with God, it begins with knowing that you need God. As it says, in John 15:5 – I can do nothing without God.

"I am the vine; you are the branches. If a man remains in me and I in him, he will bear much fruit; apart from me you can do nothing."

I had to give up trying to run my own life, to be God in my life. I am not God. I am His child. It is crazy for me to think I can know how to live life without my Creator. In order to become His child the next thing I need to do is turn away from my sins and my rebellion and ask for forgiveness for that sin, that rebellion against God.

For all have sinned and fall short of the glory of God, and are justified freely by his grace through the redemption that came by Christ Jesus.
Romans 3 v 23-24

If we confess our sins, he is faithful and just and will forgive us our sins and purify us from all unrighteousness.
John 1 v 9

The reason we can be forgiven and cleansed from all of that is because Jesus paid the penalty for your sins and mine.

He was the one who could defeat sin and the death that those sins bring. He died on a cross for you and me. He was willing to do that because He wanted us to experience the life we can have with our Heavenly Father.

For God so loved the world that he gave his one and only Son, that whoever believes in him shall not perish but have eternal life.
John 3 v 16

So we accept that gift of forgiveness and the chance to begin a relationship with our Creator. What we need to say is:

"Jesus, thank you for giving me a way to know God again. Thank you for dying on the cross for me and destroying the power of sin and death in my life. Come into my life and show me how to live."

"Here I am! I stand at the door and knock. If anyone hears my voice and opens the door, I will come in and eat with him, and he with me."
Revelation 3 v 20

Once you have given your life to God, you need to begin building a private world with Him. He has so much to teach you and show you. If you like to walk, go for a walk and talk to God about everything that is going on in your life. Listen to the Bible on your MP3 player while you walk. Write down what you feel challenged by. And then apply what you are learning to your life. Don't leave it as nice theory you are learning. Ask God to help you to live out the kind of life you read about in the Bible. Whether you like to walk or stay at home or go somewhere else, begin to bring God into every aspect of your life. Ask Him to teach you about how to make decisions, how to look at your future, what relationships to have, etc. He is your God. He wants to teach you what life was meant to be about.

Become part of a church where you can study the Bible with others and pray for each other and listen to each other. Together find the calling God has put on your life.

When you give your life to God through Jesus His son, you have an incredible life waiting for you. I cannot begin to tell you how grateful I am to God for the relationship He has given me with Him. He is the one who has given me hope. He leads me day by day in His beautiful plan for my life. Best of all, I have the Almighty God walking alongside me in every step I take and that will never, ever change.

True Sacrifice

In Chapter One I said lives that achieve greatness always require sacrifice.

Sacrifice is what is required to have an extraordinary life. Every one of us was created for a mission and to do something important with our lives. We were not created to just live selfishly and surround ourselves with material things. Jesus said that if you want to save your life you need to lose it. But if you lose your life for His sake you will save it.

True liberation and purpose comes when we deny ourselves take up our cross and follow Jesus.

I won't say "Good luck" on your journey but I will say "God bless you and lead you".

Bonus Chapter - Gifts and Abilities Part 2

We all want happiness, enjoyment, success and fulfillment in our lives. It is my belief that we each have God given gifts and abilities. We are called to nurture and grow these gifts and abilities in order to live our lives to our full potential. This in turn naturally leads to happiness, joy and success.

We are all made in God's image, and we all have a part of God's character and personality in us. If we live that God-given characteristic, we will make the world a better place as well as having an abundant life. If everyone lived their calling, the world would be a beautiful place – heaven on earth.

The important point is that our gifts and abilities guide us towards God's character in us and God's calling on our lives. It is an absolutely essential requirement of your life that you find and gravitate towards your God-given gifts and abilities.

Your gifts and abilities tell you about your destiny. It is my conviction that you can never live what you were destined to do on this earth if you don't follow after your gifts and abilities. God has given you these gifts for a purpose. That is part of the way He made you.

I also firmly believe that every person is on earth for a purpose and no other person on the planet can achieve what God has put you on earth to achieve. This says a number of things to me:

1. If you don't achieve your destiny, what you are supposed to do on earth won't get done – by anyone!

2. We need to live our lives helping others to achieve their destiny. By definition this will make the world a better place.

3. It is grossly unacceptable that tens of thousands of people every day are dying of malnutrition and preventable disease. We who are politically and economically able need to do what we can to stop this loss of human destiny.

4. If every life contains the seeds of a destiny only that specific life can achieve, it is a terrible mistake to take the life of an unborn child. Their destiny is activated the moment the spark of life is created at conception.

We were not created to have mediocre lives. God did not put part of His personality in us so we could just get by.

In John 10 v 10 Jesus said *"I have come that they may have life, and that they may have it more abundantly."*

If you are not living an abundant life and you are not living life to the full, you are not living the way you were created to live. God's purpose in creating you was for you to live the life He designed you to live and thereby experience a full and abundant life.

Sadly, individuals who are not living their God given gifts make the world a worse place to live in. If everyone lived the life they were designed by God to live, the world would be a wonderful place with every person's needs taken care of.

Bonus Chapter - My Purpose and My Why

As a follower of Jesus my purpose is two-fold; to try to be more like Jesus; and to build the Kingdom of God.

The first part is a personal journey of prayer, reading the Bible, surrender to God, obedience to Him and so on.

The second part is recognizing that for some reason God has decided to use human beings to do his work on earth. In my opinion, building the Kingdom of God means doing anything that God would do if he hadn't decided to leave the work to us. This includes:

- Fighting injustice and oppression;
- Helping the poor and marginalized;
- Supporting mission;
- Serving others;
- Helping people in need;
- Building God's church (i.e. people); and so on.

Clearly one person can't do all of these things simultaneously, which is why each of us has different gifts, abilities and passions. You will find you gravitate towards the things you care about. We are all wired differently and this is how God sets about to achieve his purpose through us. If everyone on earth fulfilled God's purpose for their life, the world would be the perfect place it was created to be. Unfortunately most people do not seek God's purpose, let alone live it.

I find myself drawn more towards helping those in need. For this reason I financially support Amnesty International, Greenpeace and World Vision for example. The first two are secular organizations and do not include God in their vision or mission, but in my opinion they are doing (at least most of the time) God's work on earth. I believe every person is made to fulfill a higher purpose than improving their own life. Regardless of your beliefs about God, you need to find your purpose. We can only be truly content if we find our true purpose in life and live that life.

Bonus Chapter - Words and Self Talk Part 2

Self talk is a critical part of our spiritual life as well.

In Genesis Chapter 1 God *spoke* the world into existence, for example verse three "*And God **said**, "Let there be light," and there was light.*" It therefore follows that because we are made in the image of God, our words are powerful and effective in making things happen in the world and in our own lives. This extends to our circumstances and the lives of those around us.

We shouldn't be surprised that as sons and daughters of God we can use our words and our self talk to create our reality.

People who are familiar with the Bible will know this. Let's look at some examples:

Pleasant words are a honeycomb, sweet to the soul and healing to the bones.
Proverbs 16 v 24

Positive words are good for your soul and can even bring healing.

From the fruit of his lips a man is filled with good things.
Proverbs 12 v 14

Positive words can fill up a person with good things on the inside.

…we take captive every thought to make it obedient to Christ.
2 Corinthians 10 v 5

We need to ensure that all of our thoughts (many of which are self talk) are thoughts that are in line with Jesus' teaching and life.

The good man brings good things out of the good stored up in his heart, and the evil man brings evil things out of the evil stored up in his heart. For out of the overflow of his heart his **mouth speaks***.*
Luke 6 v 45

Our mouths speak out what is truly in our hearts. If we are positive, encouraging and loving, that will come through in our words. In this way we actively make the world a better place.

"I tell you the truth, whatever you bind on earth will be bound in heaven, and whatever you loose on earth will be loosed in heaven."
Matthew 18 v 18

Our words are so powerful they can have an impact on the spiritual world, not just the physical world.

"Again, I tell you that if two of you on earth agree about anything you ask for, it will be done for you by my Father in heaven."
Matthew 18 v 19

And:

"The prayer of a righteous man is powerful and effective."
James 5 v 16

When we pray, we are speaking out words that have real power. Prayer is therefore a powerful way of changing the world, as well as our own hearts.

Most of us are familiar with King David's famous Psalm 23. It is pure self talk:

The Lord is my shepherd (verse 1)
I shall not want (verse 2)
He leads me beside still waters (verse 2)
He restores my soul (verse 3)
I will fear no evil (verse 4)
My cup overflows (verse 5)
Surely goodness and love will follow me all the days of my life (verse 6)

And again in Psalm 18:

He brought me out into a spacious place (verse 19)
With my God I can scale a wall (verse 29)
He enabled me to stand on the heights (verse 33)
My arms can bend a bow of bronze (verse 34)
You stoop down to make me great (verse 35)
You broaden the path beneath me (verse 36)

As spiritual beings we have to be exceptionally aware of our words and our self talk because they powerfully impact us and the people around us.

Suggestions:

1. Work to remove all negative self talk from your life.

2. Replace it with positive self talk.

3. Work to remove any negative talk about other people or situations.

4. Replace it with positive talk about others and the world around you.

5. Pray regularly and remember that when you pray, you are powerfully impacting yourself and the world around you.

Bonus Chapter - Bad Times and Challenges Part 2

During my most challenging year in 2006, in a moment of spiritual epiphany I got on my knees and told God that all I had was His, and if He wanted to take me to bankruptcy I would still love Him and still try my best to serve Him. I said this in all soul-based honesty and looking back it was a key moment in my life. I believe I have a God-given gift to make money, and it was important that I gave this part of my life to God fully and without reservation. It has cemented the fact that all I have belongs to God, and I am happy to be a conduit or a pipeline for God's money rather than hold reservoirs of money for myself.

While a spiritual breakthrough is wonderful it does not pay the bills. It doesn't even necessarily give a light at the end of the tunnel. I still had no money or any certainty the situation would change.

Fortunately I had two other positive spiritual encounters. Once when I was praying, I felt God saying to me that He was deliberately holding back the progress I was hoping for. But when the time was right, the dominoes would start to fall one after the other.

The second encounter was when a friend who hears from God in a very clear way prayed for me. I hadn't seen him for some months, and he had no idea what I had been through. When he prayed, he said I had been through a very difficult time but God was in it all, and the time would come to an end soon.

Of course "soon" was not a time period I could plan with, and I had no idea how the situation would resolve itself. However I did feel more peaceful, and it did feel good to have it confirmed that God was in the situation and not abandoning me to whatever might come along.

After I had a chance to think and pray about it, I felt God was saying to me that I had made a mistake by taking a humanistic view of my financial goals. I had been reading a lot of self-help and motivational books which had caused me to stop thinking about what God would want me to do, but rather what I could achieve on my own. I have now learned that what I need to ask is "Lord, here is my life, what do you want me to achieve for you and your kingdom this year?"

The scripture *"Unless the Lord builds the house its builders labor in vain"* (Psalm 127 v 1) came to mind many times.

I also believe I was not in a state for God to use me in a significant financial way until I had really deep down inside surrendered my finances to God. I believe that one of my main purposes on earth is to make money to further God's kingdom. I believe God had to break my humanistic ideas of making money and I had to surrender everything to Him before I was ready to be released into the calling He has for me. Interestingly 2007 and 2008 were by a huge margin the best years I have ever had financially. They would not have been possible without the difficulties of 2006. And I know that with the blessing of God, much greater things are going to happen in the years ahead.

I also know that if God took me down to zero I would be happy and content, and I would love Him just as much as if He decides to use me as a conduit for a billion dollars.

Bonus Chapter - The Law of Attraction

You may have watched the movie "The Secret" or read the book. Even if you haven't you have almost certainly heard of the "Law of Attraction".

The Law of Attraction states that life does not just happen to you. Rather you can shape and even create what happens to you by attracting to yourself the life you desire. The basic premise is that in the "universe" like attracts like, and your thoughts attract and actually manifest real situations, people, material things etc into your everyday reality. So the more you think about and focus on something the more you will attract it to yourself and the more likely it will come to pass.

So we have the following sayings:

"What you think about you bring about."

"Where focus goes, reality grows."

But the fact is the movie and the book "The Secret" are only part of the truth.

So let me be clear about what I believe:

1. There is without question a Law of Attraction that operates in the universe.

2. Like all universal laws, the law of Attraction is a God-given law that the movie and the book "The Secret" have humanized, mystified, and secularized.

Let me explain the biblical principles behind the Law of

Attraction. You will be able to see clearly where this universal principle came from.

1. Creativity

We are all created in God's image. This means we have the same characteristics as God himself. One of those key characteristics is that we have been created with the ability to ourselves create. We are beings who have creativity and the ability to create new physical things, as well as creating our own situations and our reality.

2. Prayer

Jesus teaches that we can alter the world around us and our own reality through prayer. One day the disciples asked Jesus how they should pray. Wouldn't that be a fantastic thing to know? Well Jesus answered them and gave us "the Lord's prayer."

A key part of that prayer is:

"Your kingdom come, your will be done, on earth as it is in heaven."
Matthew 6 v 10

This is exactly the spiritual law of attraction at work. Praying this prayer to God means focusing your attention on changing things on earth so they are like things in heaven – peace, joy, abundance, fulfilment, and so on.

And again, even more clearly:

Jesus said "Therefore I tell you, whatever you ask for in prayer, believe that you have received it, and it will be yours."
Mark 11 v 24

3. Bringing Things Into Existence

The Bible even recommends believing, imagining and focusing on situations you want, even if they do not exist now. Consider this verse:

"...the God who gives life to the dead and calls things that are not as if they were."
Romans 4 v 17

God can "call things that are not [i.e. don't exist now] as if they were [as if they did exist]" – and by so doing, bring them into existence.

So if God can do it and we are made in his image, it stands to reason that we too can bring things into existence that do not exist now.

4. Practical Law of Attraction Advice From the Bible

Because the Bible is filled with God's wisdom and instruction to us on how to live our lives, we should expect practical advice on how to utilize this universal law in our lives. Here are some examples:

"Finally, brothers, whatever is true, whatever is noble, whatever is right, whatever is pure, whatever is lovely, whatever is admirable—if anything is excellent or praiseworthy—think about such things."
Philippians 4 v 8

Just pure advice to focus, concentrate and think about things that are good, pure and positive.

"For as he thinks in his heart, so is he."
Proverbs 23 v 7

A clear instruction that what you think about, becomes who you are!

"The good man brings good things out of the good stored up in his heart, and the evil man brings evil things out of the evil stored up in his heart. For out of the overflow of his heart his mouth speaks."
Luke 6 v 45

Once again a crystal clear instruction that when you store up good things in your heart, it manifests in good things in your reality. Yes we really can "bring good things out of the good stored up in [our] hearts"! We can actually bring good things into existence simply because of the good that is in our heart. Of course the opposite is also true, so be very careful what you store up in your heart.

"I tell you the truth, if anyone says to this mountain, 'Go, throw yourself into the sea,' and does not doubt in his heart but believes that what he says will happen, it will be done for him."
Mark 11 v 23

Wow! There is literally no limit to what we can manifest in reality if we:

a) Really believe it; and
b) Speak it into existence.

I am excited just thinking about what I can bring into existence!

"Remember this: Whoever sows sparingly will also reap sparingly, and whoever sows generously will also reap generously."
2 Corinthians 9 v 6

This is true in your mind as well as in your actions. If you sow positive thoughts, feelings and attitudes, you will reap in the same fashion.

Okay that is the end of the Bonus Chapters.

Now on with the book…

Chapter 49 - The Hero Test

What if all of your heroes and role models arrived at your house today and looked at every area of your life?

Would you be delighted with what they found, or would you be embarrassed?

The great thing about role models and heroes is that we aspire to be more like them, and that in itself makes us want to be more and achieve more.

Asking myself this question, I thought about some of the areas of my life that I would want to hide from my heroes. Nothing terrible, just things I know I could do much better.

That also got me thinking about what standard I should try to achieve. I remember reading once that we should always strive for excellence but not for perfection. The reason is simple, perfection is almost always unattainable and if we strive for perfection itself it will take a disproportionate amount of time and energy. Here is a practical example:

I recorded over 70 videos for my website www.LifestyleBook.com. They took me about 200 hours to write, prepare, record, re-record, edit etc. I strove for excellence. However if I had been happy only with perfection, it would have taken me more like 1,000 hours and yes they would have been better, but still not perfect. And just like you, I don't have an extra 800 hours just sitting around waiting for me to fill them up.

Conclusion:

1. It is a fantastic exercise to stop for five minutes and imagine all of your heroes (and heroines) and role

models coming to your house today and looking at every area of your life:

- your health;
- your fitness;
- your wealth;
- your relationships;
- your career;
- the state of your house and your office;
- the state of your spiritual life;
- how much giving, serving and contributing you are doing for others;
- and so on.

How would you feel? Delighted or embarrassed?

2. Strive for Excellence in everything you do.

NEVER settle for mediocrity, that is the worst state of all.

But also do not drive yourself to achieve perfection. It is not an efficient use of your time.

Chapter 50 - The Absolute Fail-Safe Way to Lose Weight, Get Fitter, Be Healthier and Look Sexier!

- Eat less.
- Eat healthier.
- Exercise more.

Chapter 51 - Exercise and Diet

Okay I admit I designed the last chapter to have a chapter title longer than the chapter itself. The reason is simply to cause you to pause and remember that although there is a publishing empire based around dieting and fitness, the keys are that simple!

Given it is so simple, what keeps most people from being a healthy weight and exercising 3-4 times a week?

Simple: time and priority.

Time

Time is a huge part of what this book is about. As you cut out of your life the time-wasting activities and start building your career and other activities around your lifestyle, you will find you have the time for the important activities in life.

Priority

Prioritizing all of the many activities of modern day life is also a focus of this book. As you set goals and think about what really is important in life, you will naturally find your priorities stay at the top of your list and the irrelevancies drop off.

To give yourself additional leverage, here are the benefits of a lifestyle that includes adequate exercise and a healthy diet:

Benefits of Exercise:

- Helps to manage your weight.
- Promotes better sleep.

- Combats some serious illnesses, for example heart disease.
- Reduces depression and anxiety.
- Reduces blood pressure.
- Increases bone density which is critical in later life.
- Tones muscle.
- Enhances stamina in the workplace and in sport performance.
- Improves your mood.
- Increases self esteem.
- Reduces stress.

In the industrialized world literally tens of millions of people suffer from illnesses and disabilities that can be eliminated through regular exercise.

Benefits of a Healthy Diet:

- Strengthens your immune system.
- Prevents and treats disease.
- Leads to higher energy levels.
- Helps to manage your weight.
- Promotes better sleep.
- Promotes a longer life.
- Improves your skin, hair, teeth, nails i.e. your looks!
- Reduces mood swings and increases a feeling of wellbeing.
- Increases the ability to focus and concentrate.

Your body can only be as healthy as the fuel you give it to run on. Use the internet or visit a nutritionist for specific advice on diet and nutrition.

Exercising regularly and eating healthily are an investment in your lifestyle and a gift you can give yourself. We are blessed with the ability to exercise and eat healthily – it is a crime to avoid it.

Be disciplined, make time and make it a priority. You will never regret it.

An Important Note About Caffeine

I used to be a Connoisseur of Coffee. I had an $8,000 Italian espresso machine in my office (just for me). I used the freshest beans and made terrific coffee. I had two double shots of coffee every day, and enjoyed every aspect of it. Now I don't drink coffee and here is why:

My day started with me needing my coffee hit to "get me going". It worked great until about 1pm when I began to fade, so I had my afternoon coffee to "get me going" again. About 6pm I started to fade again but I couldn't have another coffee because then I wouldn't be able to get to sleep. My evenings were characterized by low energy and sometimes even a lie-down. By 9pm I was shutting down and no use to anyone. I generally slept okay, but not deeply. I found I needed nine hours in bed to get enough rest.

After doing some research on caffeine I realized this up and down cycle was caused by my caffeine intake. My "ups" were chemically induced! Amazingly drinking coffee was actually causing me less overall energy and stimulation! I stopped drinking coffee to trial it for a month. Admittedly for the first three days I felt very weird, but after that I started to feel fine. After a month I had a lot more energy throughout the day. I was also sleeping more deeply (caffeine builds up in your body and takes a long time to work its way out) and therefore I didn't need as many hours in bed.

I know that for many people coffee it a critical part of getting through each day and a big part of socializing but you must realize it is coming at a huge cost. If you drink coffee regularly and suffer from any of the following, I strongly suggest you give up all caffeine for a month as a trial:

- Feeling drowsy in the morning (before coffee);
- Feeling drowsy a few hours after having a coffee;
- Feeling sleepy in the late afternoon or early evening;
- Poor sleep patterns, not sleeping deeply or waking up tired;
- Not having the energy you had as a teenager (before your caffeine habit).

Trial it for a month, you have got nothing to lose. I went from Espresso-man to Water-man, and I will never go back. The cost is too high.

Remember, most soda drinks contain large amount of caffeine. It's not just coffee.

Coffee has become an acceptable social drug. It's legal, not physically addictive, and its "cool". Unfortunately, it is taking energy and strength out of your day – every day.

Chapter 52 - Your Body is a Temple

It amazes me how many people abuse the single most fundamental part of what our mind, heart and soul are encased in – our bodies!

So many people fill their bodies with known toxins and poisons:

- Nicotine (is a poison to the human body).
- Alcohol (is a poison to the human body).
- Excess fat.
- Excess sugar (is a poison to the human body).
- Preservatives, additives and food colourings (poison to the human body).
- Chemicals, pesticides and industrial toxins (poison to the human body).

Then there are people who I can't understand at all who are happy to put illicit drugs into their bodies. These are drugs that have never been tested, where there are no safety standards, where there are no standardized doses, where no side-effects have been studied or classified under scientific conditions, and where the chain of supply is filled with greedy criminals who don't care one tiny bit for the final consumer!

Can I put it any more clearly than this: You are stark raving mad if you take illicit drugs.

You only get one body; it is the temple of your soul. Even God is willing to dwell there. If you truly treat your body like a temple, it will serve you well for decades. If you abuse it you must be prepared for poor health and a lack of energy.

If this chapter has made you think seriously about the way you treat your body, read the chapter on discipline and the action steps to make immediate changes.

Did you know the Bible describes your body as a temple of the Holy Spirit?

Do you not know that your body is a temple of the Holy Spirit, who is in you, whom you have received from God?
1 Corinthians 6 vs 19

Critical Principle 11:   **Your body is a temple. Treat it as such.**

Chapter 53 - Three Keys to Health

If you want to live a spectacular life, it helps a lot if you have a lot of energy and if you have excellent health.

In simple terms the human body has three vital needs:

1. Oxygen

Without oxygen our brains die within minutes. Oxygen is also vital for the life of every cell in our bodies. It makes sense that oxygenating our bodies correctly is a critical part of our health. Unfortunately many people do not oxygenate (breathe) properly or exercise regularly, which means our bodies are not in the habit of taking in enough oxygen. When we don't breathe properly our brain function is limited. An excellent example is when you are trying to think of someone's name, when you absolutely know their name but you can't remember it. Sometimes this is caused by lack of oxygen to the brain.

Let me explain. If the brain has less than optimal oxygen, it will put all of the oxygen it receives into critical functions (keeping you alive). It takes oxygen away from non-critical areas such as memory, alertness and additional energy. If you are skeptical, try it yourself. Next time you have a "memory blank" (for example someone's name), stand up and take three or four really deep breaths and then try it. You will be amazed how often you will remember the person's name immediately.

The scope of this book does not allow in-depth analysis of oxygenation. However I recommend you:

- Research breathing exercises;

- Do aerobic exercise at least three times a week;
- Deliberately breathe deeply when you need to concentrate (for example exams, driving);
- Make deep breathing part of your morning meditation.

2. Water

Without water our bodies die within a few days. Hydration is second only to oxygen in importance for our bodies. Most people do not drink enough water. We need around 2.5 liters of water per day for optimal hydration. A good rule of thumb is that if your urine has any color in it at all, you are dehydrated. Drink enough so your urine is always clear. If you ever have a dry mouth you are severely dehydrated.

Because the longest you go without water is when you are asleep, you should always have a big drink of water as soon as you wake up. This is a very simple way of giving your body what it needs.

It's cheap, it's easy and it's good for you – drink lots of water!

Incidentally caffeine is a diuretic (its net effect is to take water out of your system) – bad!

3. Nutrition

Without food our bodies die in about six weeks. Clearly nutrition is the third most important key to life.

One small section cannot do justice to the world of nutrition. However from my extensive reading and research I will offer my suggestions on eating in the healthiest way possible:

- The closer to nature your food is, the better it will be for you.
- Home-grown and raw top the list. Start a home vegetable garden if you can.
- Try not to eat anything your grandmother would never have heard of (read the ingredient list of products at your supermarket to see what I mean).
- The more processed the item, the worse it is for you.
- Almost all fast food is detrimental to your health.
- In general we eat too much meat and not enough fresh fruit and vegetables.
- The longer you cook food, the more nutrients and vitamins are neutralized (killed) in the process.
- Good fats are good for you and we need to make sure we get enough of them. Bad fats are really bad. Research and understand the difference between the two. I recommend the book "Fats that Heal, Fats that Kill" by Udo Erasmus.
- The published food pyramid is decades out of date and needs to be fully re-written.
- The lack of vitamins in much of the soil used to grow our fruit and vegetables is so depleted that in many cases even if we eat well we are not getting enough vitamins.

Nutrition is a key to you and your family's health. If you want to live a long and healthy life, take time to understand your food and don't take short-cuts.

If you are tired and run down a lot, and you get too many colds and the flu, you may need to take particular note of this section.

One Month Challenge

I issue this challenge to you because it is a challenge I took up, and it changed my life and probably my longevity. Since I took up this challenge I have made major changes to my diet which has given me at least 30% more energy every day. I feel healthier and stronger. Also I used to get about four colds and sore throats a year. Since changing my diet, I have had one very minor cold that lasted four days. Interestingly it started the day after I had a big dinner that was completely outside these guidelines!

The challenge is only for one month. You can do anything for one month, so I suggest you are strict for the month and then decide what works for you and what doesn't.

The Challenge – One Month

No alcohol.
No caffeine.
No junk food.
No processed cookies and cakes.
No meat (fish and seafood are okay).
No dairy products (i.e. no milk or cheese).
No eggs.
Eat as much of your fruit and vegetables as you can raw.
Drink at least four pints (two and a half liters) or water (not juice) every day.
Only eat wholemeal breads.
Minimize processed foods.
Take a daily multivitamin tablet.

If you are unsure what and how to eat, there are thousands of recipes and ideas on the internet.

Remember you can do **anything** for one month. And you might find that the energy and health benefits change your life.

Chapter 54 - Discipline

If there is one attribute that stops people from achieving all life has to offer them, it is discipline. Most of the time people gravitate towards what feels good rather than what is good for us. People sleep-in rather than getting up early, eat unhealthy food that tastes good, go for a beer rather than going to the gym, watch TV rather than reading a motivating book. However, highly successful people are disciplined in their habits. Discipline is not something you are born with, it is simply a decision you make.

In order to achieve discipline, you need to take a number of decision steps. But don't be put off! If you invest a short amount of time, the pay-off in what you achieve in your life will amount to a return of thousands of percentages.

What follows is a method you can use to change undisciplined behaviors into disciplined ones.

Let's work through a practical example of one area of your life you want discipline in and follow the required steps. You can apply these steps to any area of your life.

Let's choose watching TV as our example.

Here are the action steps:

1. Give yourself leverage

You need to motivate yourself to change by listing the reasons for making the change i.e. give yourself leverage. For example, list all the bad things that will happen if you **don't** change.

Let's assume you watched 20 hours of TV last week. Here is how your leverage list might look:

- I don't have enough time in my life so how dare I waste 20 hours watching TV.
- Most of what I watched was rubbish and things I now can't even remember.
- Every time I watched the news I felt bad and sad.
- I can easily pick up the important news on the internet in five minutes a day.
- I wish I had spent that 20 hours doing what is much more important to me, for example learning the guitar, reading a motivating or educational book or exercising.
- Our family talks less and connects less when the TV is on.
- I hate the advertising and the subliminal messages they give to my kids about body shape and consumerism.

2. Make a mind-shift

Keep giving yourself leverage until you get to a point where you say to yourself "ENOUGH". "I am wasting the most important asset of my life which I will never get back – time. I have to make a change."

3. Make a decision

In the end discipline is simply a decision. If you give yourself the leverage and make the mind-shift, the decision is easy.

Your decision might be:

"Right, I am disconnecting the TV aerial and couriering the cable to my brother with strict instructions that he is to keep it for one month. We will trial no TV for one month and then we will all decide after that if we want it back. We will keep the DVD player and allow select DVDs to be played."

4. Take action NOW

As soon as you make the decision, act now while you have the leverage and the mind shift. Disconnect the TV immediately and package the cable up.

5. Set a Goal

Even taking action is not enough. Ensure you also set a goal and write it down. Your goal might be:

No matter what, I am not going to watch TV for one month.

6. Create a Habit

Now you have taken action and set a goal you need to create a new habit. If you used to watch TV after dinner, use that time to practice your guitar or interact with your family. If you used to watch TV before bed, use that time to read. You may want to set a goal for the extra time you now have in your life.

You create a habit by repeating the action or behavior over and over until it is part of your life.

Action Step 15:

Pick the one habit or situation you want to change and go through each of the steps.

Here they are again:

1. Give yourself leverage;
2. Make a mind-shift;
3. Make a decision;
4. Take action NOW;
5. Set a Goal;
6. Create a habit.

If you want to achieve your goals, be all you can be and create the lifestyle you want, you must have discipline as a core part of how you live. Think about some of the areas in your life where you lack discipline, for example: exercise, bad habits, what you eat, sleeping too long. If you work through the action steps as described you can turn these areas around.

Chapter 55 - Saying "No"

Few people are good at saying "No". We generally want to please other people and for them to like us. Unfortunately because there is so much to do and achieve in our busy lives, saying "Yes" to more activities is often a mistake. The reason it is a mistake is that over-commitment leads to stress and a lack of focus. You simply cannot do 30 activities in a week and expect to focus and achieve in all of them. If you try to squeeze too much into your life, the really important things get marginalized or left out altogether.

For example, many people say their kids, their marriage and their faith are vitally important to them. But the truth is that in many cases the kids don't get quality time, the spouses hardly see each other and prayer is something you do when you desperately need something!

How can we solve this problem?

1. List your real priorities.

2. Set disciplined goals, for example:

"I will always go to Johnny's soccer practice and take him for a milkshake afterwards."

"As a couple we will have an unbreakable date together every Thursday night."

"I will read one chapter of the Bible and pray for ten minutes every day."

3. Say "No" to anything that will get in the way of your priorities or achieving your goals.

I remember when I was trying to get really good at playing the guitar I would sometimes disappoint my friends on a Friday night when they wanted me to go to the movies with them – I just said "No". Sometimes when I set aside time to write, a friend may want to come over. I have to say "No". On Saturday mornings in Winter I take my kids to soccer, anything else gets a "No". On Tuesday evenings I pray. Everyone knows there is no point expecting me to do anything else that night. The answer will be "No!"

Chapter 56 - XXXX Yourself!

What comes to mind when you read these words:

Salesman
Salesperson
Selling

I have deliberately left a space so you can write down your thoughts in the space below, or at least pause and think about your response.

Go ahead make a note of the things that come to mind:

Salesman   Salesperson   Selling

Chances are you came up with a mostly negative list. Here are some typical responses:

- Used cars
- Life Insurance
- Pushy
- Rip-off
- Sleazy
- Greedy
- Boring
- Cold-calling
- Stressful
- Dishonest
- Unethical

Isn't it interesting? Almost everyone is programmed to believe that sales and selling are negative concepts. Let me show you that your programming is not reality and in fact deep down you believe the opposite.

Remember when you were first dating? You wore your best clothes, shined your shoes, spent hours checking your hair in the mirror, cleaned the car etc? Guess what? You were "selling yourself" to your date.

Remember when you went for your first serious job interview? You did all the same things as above but in addition maybe you learned about the company and its products. And how much time did you spend on your resume? You were selling yourself to your prospective employer.

Remember your first important school assignment? You made it neat, you proof read it, you stapled it perfectly. You were selling your skills and abilities to your teacher.

Remember going to the bank for your first loan?

Remember meeting your spouse's parents for the first time?

Remember your first client phone call?

Remember your first client meeting?

The fact is, you and I are selling ourselves to others in every professional and social situation we engage in! I would go as far as to say the level of satisfaction you have in the following is a direct reflection of how good you are at selling yourself to others:

- Your annual income.
- The quality of your peers.
- The quality of your friends and the number of friends you have.
- Your community status.
- Your love life.
- Your career.
- The parties you are invited (or not invited) to.
- The way your friends treat you.
- The way your family treats you.
- The way strangers treat you.

We have to rid our minds of any negative associations we have to selling, and we need to embrace it! You already have a long history of selling, so keep doing it and keep getting better at it.

I have a number of rules I live by:

- Nothing leaves my office unless it is absolutely as good as it can be. That includes letters, emails, documents, phone calls – everything.

- When I meet with a client or have business meetings I am always immaculately presented in the appropriate dress code.

- I am never late to meetings.

- I always reply to emails, phone messages and letters promptly and in a professional and courteous manner.

- I am always polite in all forms of communication. It is not unusual for me to send a two paragraph email with five "please" and "thank yous" – it doesn't cost anything and it makes people feel appreciated.

- I often give gifts to people I am meeting with, especially if they have given up their time to meet with me.

There are a hundred ways to effectively sell yourself to all of the people you meet or see.

Remember, if you are dissatisfied with any area of your interpersonal life it is probably because you are not selling the most important product you can ever sell – YOU!

By the way the title of this chapter is Sell Yourself! I couldn't put that at the beginning of the chapter because I needed to surprise you with your reaction to the words Salesman, Salesperson and Selling!

Now that I have outlined how important it is to sell yourself, here are some quick tips for selling in business:

Tip #1   In business Sales = Income.

Tip #2   Before you buy a product in business, know how you will sell it.

Tip #3   If you contact just five people a day to sell them your product or service you will be incredibly successful.

Tip #4   Every successful business is good at selling. If selling is not your strength get personal coaching.

Tip #5   If you are part of an organization, **everyone** in the organization has to "sell" i.e. everyone must be a good advertisement for the business.

Tip #6   Successful selling requires energy. In a selling encounter the person with the most energy always wins the sale. If you have kids you already know this is true!

Chapter 57 - Lies You Have Been Told

It is an unfortunate truth the more often we hear something, the more likely we are to believe it. In fact we are prone to absorbing frequently-told lies and believing them. The problem is these lies rob us of opportunities and choices. This of course limits our ability to create our Perfect Lifestyle.

What follows are a number of widely believed statements that are simply not true. Like any good lie however, there is a grain of truth in them.

Lie 1   There is no such thing as a free lunch.

Truth 1   There are **a lot** of cheap lunches out there.

The Lie is this:

Life is hard and you don't get anything for nothing. You have to work really hard for everything you get. If you find an opportunity, don't trust it because it is probably not what is seems. Do things the way they have always been done, and you won't go wrong.

The Truth is this:

Life is wonderful and it abounds with exciting opportunities. When you see an opportunity, get excited about it before someone else does. Look for the unseen angle and look for new ways to do things. It is better to work smart than to work hard.

There are a number of examples of this from my own experience. When my wife and I bought our first home it was a wreck. It had been lived in for years by two alcoholics with psychiatric problems. There were burns in the carpet, parts of the house smelled like a urinal, no maintenance had been done for decades, and it was dark and ugly inside. At the back of the house was a tiny sewing room which had low windows. If you bent double you could see a fantastic view of the harbor.

We paid $145,000 for the house, and we very quickly pulled up all of the old carpet and for $1,000 we had all of the floors polished and polyurethaned. Next we built a twenty five square yard (meter) deck out from where the sewing room used to be. This cost $5,000. Suddenly we had a light bright home with million dollar views valued at $220,000.

Another example is when I purchased an online property business in 2004. I paid $1,750 for it. The business made more than the purchase price in the first year alone giving me more than a 100% return on my investment. It took just a few hours over the whole year to manage it.

I purchased a rental property in 2002 for $270,000. The bank loaned me all of the money so I did not have to put up any cash. I found five doctors who moved in on the very day I took possession, and they paid $500 per week. This gave me an immediate Rental Return of 9.63%. Mortgage interest rates at the time were around 7%, so even though I borrowed all of the money, after paying interest and rates and insurance, I still made $50 cash every week. Now that is a cheap lunch!

My advice is look for opportunities everywhere. Look for the unseen angle. Look for the cheap lunches. There are a lot of them out there!

Lie 2　　　To be successful you have to be in the right place at the right time.

Truth 2A　　You will naturally be in the right place at the right time at least six times a year.

Truth 2B　　Put yourself in the right place more often.

Truth 2C　　Teach yourself to recognize when you are in the right place at the right time.

The Lie is this:

It is only lucky people who are successful. They are people who happen to be in the right place at the right time. They heard a tip, or were given a chance no-one else had access to. You can't do anything to improve your chances.

The Truth is this:

Yes there are situations where it is advantageous to be in a certain place at a certain time. But by natural probability alone you will be in such a situation at least once every two months. If you had seen and taken advantage of just half of the opportunities you were given, you would be a lot closer to your Perfect Lifestyle. With the gift of hindsight you will recognize this! The good news is you can learn how to get yourself into the right place at the right time so these opportunities arise not just six times a year but sixty times a year! Also you can learn to recognize the good opportunities from the not so good ones.

So how do you put yourself in the right place more often? There are lots of ways depending on what sort of opportunities you are looking for. One example is when I was in my early twenties, and I wanted to be a rock star. I played my electric guitar all the time until I was good enough, and then I put an advertisement in the newspaper looking for other musicians to form a band. Another guitar player and a bass player replied and we found a singer and a drummer. Unfortunately I never became a rock star, but I gave myself the best chance. Contrast that with a guy I knew who was a drummer. He hadn't played in a band for years, and I asked him "Why aren't you playing in a band?" He replied "Oh something will come along." He was wrong. Nothing did come along, and let's be honest nothing is likely to "come along". You have to go out and find things, and make things happen.

Once again the purchase of one of my online Real Estate competitors was an example of this. Two years after I purchased my business I found out who all my competitors were, and I emailed them all saying if ever they were interested in selling their business to contact me. Six months later, the owner of one of them emailed me to say she wanted to sell. If I had never sent that email it is very unlikely I would have even known about her plans.

Another example is my first ever teacher placement in my recruitment company. I had been trying unsuccessfully for months to place a teacher in England. I had a few teachers on my books and a few schools that had agreed my terms of business. A school in Reading, just out of London, emailed me to say they needed a PE teacher as soon as possible. Unfortunately I had no PE teachers on my books. At this stage it would have been easy to just email the school back to tell them I was sorry but I did not have a teacher for them. But this would have been falling into the trap of thinking I just wasn't in the right place at the right time.

Instead what I did was phone every College of Education in the country and I asked to speak to the Head of the Secondary program. I told each of the people I talked to that I had a great position in England for a PE teacher and asked whether they knew of any recent graduates who hadn't found a job who might be interested. Within twenty four hours a teacher I had never heard of, and who had never heard of me phoned me about the position. By the end of the week the school had the teacher's Resume, they held a telephone interview and the placement was made. I had to hustle and I had to get out of my comfort zone. But I was desperate to make a placement and I changed the situation to put myself in the right place at the right time.

Of course when my business got established, and I had literally thousands of teachers and hundreds of schools, I found I was often "in the right place at the right time". One of the best examples was when I received the Resume of a young teacher who taught History and Music. Exactly two days later a school emailed me asking for a History and Music teacher. It took me about ten minutes to put the two of them together, and I earned thousands of dollars in fees.

In business and real estate which are areas I concentrate on, I go to lots of open homes, I attend motivational and business related seminars, and I meet with other entrepreneurs. I also talk to and listen to friends, relatives, acquaintances and so on to find new opportunities. If I am at a party, and I get chatting to someone, there's a good chance they are involved in something or have access to something I have never even thought of. This is also a great source of new opportunities. It is for this reason I maintain a large network of acquaintances. I often keep people's business cards and I almost always email people who have given me their business card, just to make contact with them. You never know when that contact will come in handy.

Action Step 16:

Always keep business cards and email addresses and websites of friends, acquaintances and casual contacts.

If you are looking for business opportunities you need to read the business news, subscribe to business magazines, read business books, look at the businesses for sale section of Ebay or the newspaper or contact business brokers. You should also use the internet to see what is happening in other countries that could open up importing opportunities.

Finally you need to always keep your ear to the ground to pick up anything of interest from anyone you meet or from anything you see or read. And of course, you need to be ready to act when you see or hear of an opportunity. You have to be willing to risk a small amount of money to give something a go. Perhaps set aside $500 or $1,000 or $50,000 dollars (whatever your budget), or be willing to borrow a certain amount of money so when an opportunity arises you can go for it.

Lie 3   The small business failure rate is very high – "three out of four small businesses fail in the first five years".

Truth 3   This failure rate is made up primarily of:

- Starry eyed dreamers.
- Unrealistic optimists.
- Naïve redundancy receivers.
- Failed musicians, artists and authors.
- Unprepared "hopers" with no plan.

The Lie is this:

So many small businesses fail you shouldn't even consider starting a small business. Failure is a terrible thing, and you should avoid going anywhere near it.

The Truth is this:

If you are prepared, it is very likely you will be successful in business. There is no such thing as failure, only learning experiences. Even if you start a business and it does not succeed, you will have learned far more about yourself, about life and about business than if you had never embarked on a business adventure.

Don't be put off by any statistic you hear about the small business failure rate. Generally the people who fail in a small business have little or no financial knowledge. If you do your homework, learn the basics of business, protect the downside and follow your passions, you are very likely to be successful.

In the last ten years, I have started five companies. Four are profitable and successful. The fifth was profitable but time consuming and did not fit into my lifestyle. I dropped it to concentrate on the other businesses.

My wife has also set up a successful and profitable small business.

Further, in the last few years I purchased two companies – one made an average of a 20% annual return, the other made over 100% annually. Both of these companies focused on real estate which I was passionate about. I have since sold both, at an excellent profit.

Am I a small business genius? No! But there are two things that set me apart from the people who fail in business. The first advantage I have is that I understand business and accounting. I have studied and I understand the following:

- Budgeting;
- Return on investment;
- Capital requirements;
- Cashflow;
- Compliance and tax;
- Presentation of financial statements to banks.

The second advantage I have is that I only involve myself in projects I am passionate about and that help to achieve my lifestyle goals. When you are excited about getting up, getting into work and finding out all about your business and the market and your competitors, it is easy to become an expert. It is fun to look for opportunities or examine any threats.

Lie 4   It is almost impossible to have a really successful small business and make a lot of money.

Truth 4   It has never been easier to be successful and make money.

The Lie is this:

If you start a small business you should expect to struggle financially, and you will be lucky to make a go of it let alone earn enough to live on, and certainly not a really good income.

The Truth is this:

If you start out with an expectation to do well, to be successful and make a great income, the chances are you will achieve just that. The small business model and attitudes of twenty years ago are out of date and unrealistic. Ecommerce and globalization give us a fantastic opportunity to start successful small businesses.

I used to think if I lived in a really big city, whatever idea I had would reach such a large potential audience that even if only a tiny percentage of people liked the idea it would be successful. So I daydreamed about living in Los Angeles and selling a new style skateboard by mail order. But now we have had the amazing good fortune that wherever you live, the world has come to you!

We have been gifted a twenty first century trifecta: Technology, The Internet and Globalization.

We have suddenly been connected to the world like never before and the rest of the world is very happy for us to provide their goods and services.

An excellent example is my international recruitment company that recruited professionals from around the world to work in England. The staff never met the candidates. They placed a teacher from Canada into England from an office in New Zealand! Changes in technology enabled a business that would not have been possible ten years ago. These types of business are internet and email based with multiple websites in different countries around the world. These businesses can use free-call 1800 numbers from those countries and calls come directly through to the Head Office. This means for example that someone in Canada can phone the agency about a job in England, and the call comes through to New Zealand.

Technology also allows the business to email 150 English teachers at the touch of a button to tell them about a new vacancy. Technology allows them to email 5,500 newsletter subscribers at the touch of a button, and automatically manage email bounce-backs. Further, you can record how many of the people who received the newsletter actually went to the website to check out the information posted there.

Another good example is a business that sells empty lots of real estate (sections). A website allows a person selling a section to list it for sale for a one off fee. Technology allows the seller to enter their own information, take their own photos, upload the photos to the website and then pay for the service using their credit card. Because the business basically runs itself, the costs are extremely low. Email allows staff to communicate quickly and efficiently with clients, and if required a client can call on the free call number. Technology allows buyers from all over the world to view properties online and contact the seller directly via email. This type of business could not exist before email and the internet.

A further example is a domain name business I started in 2003. The business buys and sells domain names. How I started this business is a good example of putting yourself in the right place at the right time.

I was looking for a domain name, and I found that a company owned it already. I went to their website and found it was a company that had registered hundreds of domain names in order to re-sell them. On the corner of the website was a note saying the business was for sale. I emailed one of the directors and we started discussing a purchase. As part of our discussions the director emailed me all of the domain names the company owned and the day each one expired. This was important because domain names cost around $10 each per year to hold and I needed to work out the cashflows.

Unfortunately for the company they wanted a huge price for the whole business and they were not willing to let me purchase the selection of names I particularly wanted. Another problem they had was there were three directors, and they could not agree on a price or a sales strategy. After a few weeks I realized the purchase was going nowhere and I pulled out. I expected someone else to buy the business, but I kept my eye on their domains just in case.

I was surprised and delighted to find that instead of selling the best names or even re-registering them, the company allowed them all to expire. So I took my list of their domains and on the day each one expired, I registered it for $10. I registered the best 100 names which cost me $1,000. Soon after I sold seven of the names for a combined value of $4,950!

I told a friend about my success and he found and registered a new name for $10 and sold it three weeks later for $700 – I couldn't believe it!

One of the main advantages of this business is the costs are low, as for most internet businesses. The second advantage is it takes almost no time at all, perhaps an hour a week. The third advantage is the margins are huge!

Lie 5   You need a lot of Capital to start a business.

Truth 5   To set up an internet business you need a PC and a phone.

The Lie is this:

You need at least tens of thousands of dollars to set up your own business because you need premises, machinery, equipment, an advertising budget and so on.

The Truth is this:

Some of the most successful small businesses in the last ten years started either from home or a small cheap office and required less than $5,000 in start-up money.

When I first started my recruitment business I rented a lounge from someone I knew for $40 a week. I had a phone, a horrible fax someone gave me because their parents were throwing it out, a computer, and a very good website designer. I also worked two days a week for my previous employer so my young family had at least a bit of money coming in until the business became profitable. My advertising budget was pathetic and allowed me to put two or three line ads in newspapers when most of my competitors were running two and three column ads in full color!

In hindsight it was a great experience because I had to think carefully about every dollar I spent, and I didn't have the luxury of doing what my competitor's did. This forced me to think about inexpensive and clever ways I could reach candidates and clients. Since then I have watched some of my competitors waste thousands of dollars while I kept a lean but sharp business running.

Lie 6   You need to diversify your portfolio.

Truth 6   You should concentrate on just a few investments or businesses.

The Lie is this:

In order to increase your wealth and your passive income and therefore improve your lifestyle you need to spread your investments across a number of different investment classes. This is to protect you from a downturn in a particular sector, and also to allow you to participate in any large gains in another sector.

The Truth is this:

Spectacular increases in wealth are made when you concentrate on and really understand one or two types of investments or businesses

Having a diversified portfolio only makes sense for people at or close to retirement age where slow and steady gains are the aim. The only other situation where it works is if you have an amount of money to invest but no time to put energy into managing it because you are earning an exceptional income elsewhere. If you are not in one of these two categories, don't buy the lie that you should spread your precious money around lots of different investments.

The reason is simple; by investing some time and energy learning about a particular type of investment you will be able to increase your wealth much faster, than by playing safe across the field.

Let's have a look at two of the wealthiest people on the planet:

Bill Gates was successful because he concentrated solely on developing software for PCs. In his first few years of business do you think he had bonds, equities, or commercial property investments? He didn't. He invested all of his time and money and attention into his business.

Warren Buffett states publicly that his investment company, Berkshire Hathaway concentrates on relatively few investments. He and his company research everything they can about a target company, management and the market, and then they buy a significant shareholding in the company. In many cases they ask for a seat on the board of directors of the target company so they can help to manage it.

Most successful investors and successful companies take this approach. For this reason companies often state publicly that they are concentrating on core business rather than looking at businesses and investment where they have no knowledge or expertise.

My advice is to research all of the business and investment opportunities open to you and choose one or two you are particularly attracted to. Once you have decided, find out everything possible about those investments. Make sure you understand them as well as you can before you invest. But remember you will do 90% of your learning by doing. So no matter how much you learn by reading books and researching, you will learn far more in your first year of actually doing the investing, or running your business.

As you will have gathered by now, the two areas I have concentrated on are real estate and online businesses. Twenty years after I bought my first rental property and twelve years after I started my first online business, these are still the two main areas I focus on. For this reason I am in a far better position than the average person to significantly increase my wealth by investing in these areas. I have also made a lot of mistakes and learned from them, so I now save myself a lot of money and hassle by not investing in some opportunities.

Critical Principle 12:   **Sometimes the best investment decision you make is not to invest.**

A good example of concentrating on one or two investment types is when I was three years out of university, working for a meager salary, but working hard to build a residential property portfolio. It was 1997, and my wife and I had a combined income of $75,000. We owned a 1984 Honda CRX worth $700, a dining table that cost $60, a TV that cost $50, and a range of other second hand furnishings. However we owned four properties with a combined value of $1.2 million. Of course we had mortgages on these properties, but the rents paid the mortgages. The great thing was that properties in the late nineties went up between 10% and 20% per year. This meant that even in a bad year our capital gains were $120,000 tax free! This was more than double our after tax income from working our butts off 40-50 hours a week.

How did we get so much property? We only concentrated on property. I found investments that were undervalued so six months after I bought them I could get a property valuation stating we had $50,000 new equity in the property. The bank was happy to loan us more money for the next property, and so on. We rode a wonderful property boom, and in four years we made half a million dollars in increased property values. In that time we had no stocks, we had no bonds, we had no businesses, and we had no cash. We just concentrated on one thing – residential investment property.

Conclusion

For me there are three key requirements for businesses I own:

- They do not take up much of my valuable time;
- They give me freedom to be where I want to be at any time of the work day; and
- They only relate to pursuits I am passionate about.

Because all of my business and investment decisions are filtered through these three requirements, I ensure my businesses meet my lifestyle goals. Your lifestyle goals and aspirations will be different to mine, but you must make sure that whatever you decide to spend your time doing, it is consistent with your overall goals for the life you want to live in the future.

It is easy to fall for sugar-coated lies, especially if they resonate with the way we have been brought up, what we learned at school, or what our peers believe. It is sometimes more comfortable to believe a lie if the truth would force us to get up and take some action to make things happen. But this is exactly what you must do if you want to avoid a mediocre life where you achieve nothing but boredom and rut-digging – stand up and take some action. Do it now!

Chapter 58 - Age Is No Barrier!

It always amazes me when people think that chronological age has anything to do with anything. Once you are an adult, say voting age, how old you are is completely irrelevant.

Some people I know are reluctant to have friends who are more than a few years away from their age – how limiting! I have really close friends who are half my age and others who are nearly twice my age.

Many people put an age limit on particular activities. How often do you hear "Oh I'm too old for that", or "That's only for young people" or "I'm getting close to retirement age" or "At my age I think I'd better slow down". Or perhaps worse "I won't be able to take that step until I'm much older", or "People don't achieve that until they are in the 50s or older."

These statements are all limiting. Your chronological age is completely irrelevant to everything.

Critical Principle 13:   **Your chronological age is completely irrelevant to everything.**

Let's look at some examples:

Nelson Mandela became President of South Africa at 75 years of age.

Fauja Singh ran a marathon in 2009 aged 98.

Ronald Reagan became the governor of California at 61, and became US President at 69.

Gandhi was 61 when he and his followers marched 240 miles in 24 days to make their own salt from the sea in defiance of British colonial laws and taxes.

Benjamin Franklin played an instrumental role in drafting and signing the Declaration of Independence when he was 70. At age 81, he signed the Constitution of the United States of America.

Frank McCourt, the author of the bestseller "Angela's Ashes" first began to write in his sixties.

Chaucer wrote the Canterbury Tales between the ages of 54 and 61.

Germany's greatest literary figure Johann Wolfgang von Goethe completed "Faust" in his eighties.

Sir Winston Churchill was 66 when he became Prime Minister of the United Kingdom.

Ray Kroc was a milkshake machine salesman until he met the McDonald brothers. In 1954 at age 52 Ray Kroc opened his first McDonalds restaurant. He was reputed to be worth $500 million when he died.

Burt Munro was a New Zealand motorcycle racer who set an under 1000cc world record at the Bonneville Salt Flats (USA) on 26 August 1967. This record still stands today. Burt Munro was 68 and was riding a 47 year old motorbike when he set his record.

At age 69 Claude Monet completed the water lily painting, Le bassin aux nympheas. The painting sold for US$61 million in 2008.

Leonardo Da Vinci completed the Mona Lisa when he was 53.

Walt Disney didn't open Disneyland until he was 54.

Jessica Tandy won an Academy Award at age 80.

No matter how "old" you think you are, your chronological age bears no relationship to what you can achieve. In fact we should be expecting to do more, achieve more, and impact the world more, the older we get. If you are just starting out in life, you need to remember this. Set goals for the next five and ten years. But in the back of your mind remember as your life progresses you should be achieving bigger, greater and more significant goals – and **definitely not** smaller and less significant goals.

In fact, a recent study by Professor Mark Hart and three colleagues at Kingston University Business School found that older entrepreneurs are more likely to succeed in business than their younger counterparts. The study showed that people between 50 and 65 are less likely to fail in business, because they generally have more self-confidence, get better treatment from the banks and have extensive experience, business contacts and assets. The report stated: "Starting or buying a small business could be one dream older people could fulfill once they have the time and resources to choose for themselves."

I like a point made by Jack Canfield in his wonderful book "The Success Principles":

"In the venture capital industry, a new statistic is emerging. If the founding entrepreneur is 55 years old or over, the business has a 73% better chance of survival. These older entrepreneurs have already learned from their mistakes. They're simply a better risk because through a lifetime of learning from other failures, they have developed a knowledge base, a skill

set, and a self confidence that better enables them to move through the obstacles to success."

You should keep this in the back of your mind as an option for the future. Your learning experiences (failures) now are preparing a foundation for your future successes.

Also of course, youth is no barrier.

J. Paul Getty made his first million dollars at age 24, and that was back in 1916 when a million dollars was a *lot* of money.

Budhia Singh ran 40 miles (more than a marathon) in 2006. He was four and a half years old.

Bill Gates started Microsoft when he was 20 years old.

Christopher Paolini became a New York Times Best Selling author at age 19 with his first book "Eragon".

Michael Dell started Dell Computers when he was 19 years old.

Marjorie Gestring won an Olympic gold medal in diving at 13 years of age.

Steve Jobs started Apple when he was 21 years old.

Lawrence Bragg was 25 years old when he received the Nobel Prize for Physics.

Tatum O'Neal won an Academy Award at age 10.

Your age is completely irrelevant. It has nothing to do with your health, your wealth, your level of achievement, your friendships, or the activities you choose to do. Birthdays are fun. You get to celebrate with your friends, eat cake and get presents. But that is the only thing birthdays are for. Never define what is possible or permissible by how many or how few candles are on your cake!

Also, the concept of "retirement" should not be part of your vocabulary. If you are in a job that requires you to retire at a particular age, start looking for an alternative. You should aim to do what you love until they carry you out in a box. If you are doing what you love there is no reason to stop doing it.

It is very important to watch your self talk as you go through life. I'm sure we all know people who literally say "I'm getting old", "I'm not as young as I used to be", I can't keep up like I used to", "At this time of my life it's time to slow down", "We're all slowly dying after age 25". These are self-damaging negative self talk statements. Your body and your nervous system absorb these words and slowly make them a reality! I deliberately do the opposite.

Two of my favorite self talk statements are:

"I'm healthy and young."

And;

"My cells are regenerating and keeping me young."

I also like statements that empower you on big scary birthdays:

"40 is the new 25."

"60 is the new 40."

"70 is the new 50."

Whatever words come out of your mouth, or whatever thoughts you think about age, make them positive and energizing.

Oh I should also add that my goal is to live in a healthy and energized state until I am 125. I tell myself this every morning, and I tell anyone who is interested. Because of this, my mind and my heart and my body are recruited into the process of keeping me young, healthy, and energetic.

Chapter 59 - How to Love Mondays

When I was a university student I had a vacation job as a factory worker in a plastics factory. The conditions were bad; the work was brain-numbing. It was one of those jobs that give you all the motivation you need to get an education.

After I got to work, I just longed for the morning tea break, after that I couldn't wait for lunch time. Then I hung out for the afternoon tea break, and finally I daydreamed about punching the clock at 4pm. The closer I got to the weekend the better I felt and Friday 4pm was relief and celebration. The weekend was great – but I dreaded Monday mornings. To think I had to do the whole grind again was demoralizing.

Of course now my life is the complete opposite. I love what I do, and I can't wait to get to my office. My work and my environment feed me energy and motivation and satisfaction.

I'm sure you already know the reasons these two situations are so different. But here's a quick summary:

- I have found a job I love doing.
- I followed what I was good at and what I enjoyed doing, and over time I found my niche.
- I deliberately set out to build a lifestyle around my work life.
- I was disciplined in setting goals and working hard to achieve them.
- When challenges arose (as they always do), I focused on where I wanted to be, not what was trying to stop me.
- I didn't waste hundreds of hours on activities that would not benefit me in the long term.

- I worked on being a great husband.
- I worked on being a great dad.
- I took my physical health, nutrition and exercise seriously.
- I made my spiritual life a priority.

None of this is rocket science, and all of it is achievable. If you set your mind to it you can achieve the lifestyle you want and deserve.

If you don't already, you can ensure that for the rest of your life you enjoy Mondays as much as every other day of the week, including vacations!

Chapter 60 - Feeling Great!

Depending on what stage you are at in life, it might be a long time since you felt really amazingly on-fire great! You might be surrounded by people you love, have a good occupation, be happy and healthy, but that's not what I'm talking about. If you are over 25 think back to a day or a feeling you had in your late teens and early twenties when you woke up and the world just sparkled.

The grass was so green it caught your breath, the sun was so warm. Your mind was so clear; you had a sense of ultimate freedom and peace. It just felt amazing to be alive. Nothing at all had to happen on that day because it was already perfect. Then your favorite song came on the radio, and your best friend dropped in and brought you a sensational sandwich and a delectable chocolate brownie. You read your book in the sun and you smiled for no reason at all except the world was a wonderful place and you were in it.

I remember days like that, don't you?

For many people these seem like memories of a different person in a different place. And the reason is, our modern lives are so full of clutter and possessions and details and career and mental baggage and disappointments and limiting beliefs and so on.

Have you ever wondered why it is we have more money, a higher standard of living, and a huge increase in personal labour saving devices compared to people in the 1950s, but we are far more busy, we work longer hours and we are less care-free?

Have you ever experienced firsthand the lives of typical people in developing countries? They have few possessions but they laugh and smile and whistle and dance far, far more than we Western city-dwellers.

This book is partly about creating or re-creating an environment in your life that brings those wonderful days back into your life regularly.

My personal experience is similar. I got too busy, too cluttered, too focused on the wrong things and without even realizing it, I stopped having those really wonderful days on a regular basis. But since I made the decision that I would plan for and set goals for creating a Perfect Lifestyle, those days have come back more and more regularly.

My hope and prayer is the same will happen to you. If your life is heavily cluttered and full of detail and baggage etc, it will take a while to unravel the web you have spun around yourself. But you must do it. Because that is where you destiny is, that is where your freedom is and that is where your Perfect Lifestyle is.

And if you are just starting out, ensure you plan your Perfect Lifestyle now before you tangle this type of web around yourself.

Feeling Great Tip #1 – Move

Most of us live sedentary lifestyles. We sit at desks, we sit in front of computers, we sit with friends, we sit and watch TV and DVDs. But one of the keys to feeling great is regular movement. If you haven't felt really great for a while, how much are you moving your body? There are lots of simple ways to move more:

- Walk. Walk with friends, with your spouse, by yourself. Always walk to the shops or the post office if within walking distance. Always walk up and down stairs in office buildings.

- Lymphasise. It is easy to bounce on a rebounder/lymphasiser while you are doing something else. I lymphasise most days in the morning to start my day.
- Forced breaks. If you have been sitting at your desk for an hour, set an alarm and force yourself to get up and walk somewhere just for two to three minutes.
- Exercise. Build regular exercise into your week. Pick an exercise you most enjoy. Remember this is not about getting fit, it's just about moving – so don't push yourself.

Feeling Great Tip #2 – Don't Move

At the other end of the scale, although we live sedentary lifestyles, we almost never take time out to just "be". When was the last time you just sat down somewhere quiet, closed your eyes and:

- Just breathed?
- Just listened?
- Just waited?
- Just meditated?
- Just prayed?

Action Step 17:

Next week make three specific changes in the amount you move. Arrange a walk, take some forced breaks, and walk up stairs instead of taking the elevator.

Action Step 18:

Next week set aside just five minutes a day to just sit in a quiet place on the floor, back straight and legs crossed (chairs and couches are too comfortable, this is not a power nap!), and breathe, listen, wait, meditate, and pray.

If after a week it has not improved how you feel, you have lost nothing! If you feel a lot better, keep doing it until it becomes a habit.

Here is a great video on longevity (nearly twenty minutes long) that confirms these two tips:

http://www.ted.com/talks/dan_buettner_how_to_live_to_be_100.html

Rules for Happiness

Some people have rules for when they allow themselves to feel happy. Here is an example:

"I can only feel happy if I am earning 10% more than last year, and I am in the top three in sales for my company, and I have exercised three times this week, and my weight has not increased since last week, and my mother has not told me she is disappointed with me, and my spouse has told me he/she loves me, and my dog has to run to greet me!"

You might have a similar list, it might even be unconscious. But if you do have a list that has to be fulfilled before you can be happy, you are making it extremely difficult to feel great. Think about whether your personal psychology is requiring you to tick certain boxes before you can allow yourself to be happy. Remember being happy and contented is a **choice**.

I used to unconsciously feel that when I was trading, I had to be trading profitably to be really happy. That is madness! By definition, on some days I am going to take losses. Why let something completely outside of my control determine my state of happiness?

In order to re-program myself I now have written on my wall:

Every day:

- I am alive;
- Have three beautiful children;
- Have a lovely wife;

-        is a GREAT day!

Chapter 61 - Just Three

There are a lot of suggestions and recommendations in this book. It might seem like a lot to take in and many changes to make. But there is a very simple technique for making change manageable.

You can transform your life with the principle I am about to outline. It is one of the key principles in this book.

First, think about where you want to be in five years time. Then pick just the one main area of your life that requires the most change in the next five years. Write it down, but be specific.

Second, write one specific five year goal for that area.

Third, make a commitment to yourself and one other person that you will complete just **three small tasks** every day to achieve your goal.

Let's look at an example. Say the one main area is your career. Say the goal you wrote down was:

In five years time I will own my own business. It will earn over $200,000 per year, and I will love what I do. But I won't work more than 15 hours a week, and I will take ten full weeks annual vacation.

Start today by taking just three small actions towards that goal. Some ideas:

1. Order the most popular book on Amazon written by someone successful in a similar business.

2. Google some ideas you have for the business.

3. Find out about a small business accounting course.

4. Email a friend for advice.

5. Register a domain name.

6. Set up one Social media site for the business.

7. Do a budget and set up a savings plan.

8. Spend five minutes writing ideas and diagrams on a standard size piece of paper.

9. Phone a friend and tell them your ideas.

10. Download a relevant free audio to your MP3 player and listen to it next time you exercise.

11. Visit a similar business and see how they do what they do.

12. Visit a website of a future competitor. Request their marketing material.

13. Send a request to a potential mentor in that field.

14. Call your bank and ask them what you should be doing ahead of time.

15. Set a goal for the first year of your business.

16. Set a date for your first sale.

17. Order a book on marketing.

18. Find ten websites that sell your planned product or service and write down what you do and don't like about the websites.

19. Get a simple website made utilizing the best features you have seen.

20. Make a plan for how you are going to move out of what you are doing now.

If you take three small actions every day, you will achieve faster and higher than you ever thought possible.

Action Step 19:

Commit to yourself and one other person that you will take three small steps every day towards fulfilling your dream.

Chapter 62 - Sixteen Tips for Making Money

Here are sixteen tips on how to make money. These tips are not "get rich quick" suggestions, rather if you follow this advice you will (over time) significantly increase your wealth.

Tip #1: Buy Low – Sell High

It seems too simple and too obvious, but it is powerfully true. If you buy and sell properties, investments, equities, or anything using this tip, you cannot go far wrong.

Everything moves in cycles, and history does repeat itself. For example, look at the Canadian dollar against the US dollar in the last six years. If you had bought the Canadian dollar at $1.60 and sold it at parity, you would have made a fortune.

Similarly if you buy property when everyone is talking doom and gloom and no-one wants to own investment properties, you will do well.

Do not buy equities (stocks) when everyone else is buying them and the market is at record highs. Similarly do not sell after a crash.

You do not need hindsight to take advantage of this tip. When you see something that is historically cheap (except individual stocks which might be going down the gurgler) for no good reason, buy. If you own something that someone is willing to pay you much more than you think it is worth, sell.

Tip #2: Buy High – Sell Higher

As a corollary to Point 1, it is sometimes profitable to buy strength and sell weakness. Often financial assets that are performing strongly continue to do well, and those that are performing poorly continue to do so.

Tip #2A: You Never Buy at the Bottom or Sell at the Top

It is helpful to remember you pretty much never buy at the very bottom of a market, or sell at the very top. As long as you get the direction and momentum right you will make money. For example, let's say you want to buy a few ounces of gold as an investment. Assume the gold price has been around US$1,500 per ounce for a few months. You wait until it goes up outside its recent trading range. Say you buy it at US$1,545 per ounce. It then builds on this momentum and gets to US$1,700 per ounce. You decide to sell at US$1,700 and in the next few weeks it reaches its peak for the year of US$1,935 per ounce. It then drops to US$1,550 per ounce. You have not purchased at the bottom and you have not sold at the top, but you got the direction and the momentum correct and you made US$155 per ounce.

This is important because it is easy to beat yourself up for not picking the "perfect" moment to buy or sell. The truth is it doesn't matter, and it is impossible to pick the exact high and low. This relates to almost every type of investment: stocks, bonds, real estate and so on.

Tip #3: When to Sell

Buying an investment is easier than selling one because once you own something you have an emotional attachment to it. This is the reason many people hold investments, for example stocks, well after they should have sold them. I have a critical test I use to help me determine if I should sell an investment:

If I had the cash right now, would I buy this investment at its current price?

If the answer to this question is "No", I need to sell my investment.

This applies to real estate, stocks, businesses, trading, gold – every investment!

Tip #4: Follow Momentums

When you see momentum building in relation to a particular market, buy into that market. If you get in early enough and take a big enough exposure, you can make a killing. Property markets, stock markets, commodity markets etc move in cycles driven by momentum. Stop buying and/or start selling when you see the momentum slowing considerably.

Tip #5: Pay your Bills *Early*

People often get this one back to front. They think that if they pay their bills as late as they can they will save a tiny bit of interest. But this is almost always counter-productive. Let's say you have a $400 bill (invoice) and your average cost of borrowing is 4%. Your bill is due on the 20th of the month but you pay two weeks late. You are saving yourself $400 x 4% x 14/365 (i.e. 14 days out of 365 days a year) = 61 cents.

Yes you are saving 61 cents! You are annoying whoever you are paying and causing bad will instead of goodwill, and you are damaging your own reputation in the community. When you need that supplier in the future, are you likely to get immediate service?

Let me give you an example. Over the years I have owned a number of rental properties. Occasionally I need plumbing or electrical work done. When I get their bill, I pay it immediately. Plumbers and electricians are busy people. But when I call them for an urgent job, do you know what? They always come fast. Why? They **know** they are going to get paid, and they know they are going to get paid fast. If there is one thing these suppliers love it is getting paid fast. It saves **me** time and money by paying my bills immediately. And of course word gets around that I am an excellent bill payer. That reputation is gold.

If you are a late bill payer, change this terrible and counter-productive habit now. It will enhance your time, your reputation and your wallet!

Tip #6: Go with Your Strengths

In any business or investment venture go with what you like and what you are good at. For example don't start a recruitment business if you don't like interacting with people. Don't buy an investment property if you can't stand real estate. Do start a business or invest in things you understand and are passionate about.

Tip #7: Go for Broke if you are Onto a Winner

If you find something that is really "hot" and you have some real successes in that area already under your belt, stop looking for something else and just concentrate on that. Put all of your energy and resources into that. Can you imagine Bill Gates starting out, spending half his time developing software and the other half running a chain of restaurants? No he just went for broke on software.

Tip #8: Think Big

One of my favorite quotes is from Donald Trump's book "The Art of the Deal":

"I like thinking big. I always have. To me it's simple: if you're going to be thinking anyway, you might as well think big. Most people think small, because most people are afraid of success, afraid of making decisions, afraid of winning. And that gives people like me a great advantage."

He is right. If you are thinking about a business or a venture have a big dream, think about what might be possible. If you have a successful business, think about franchising it or think about having a presence in every large country.

When I was at university I thought that if only I could think of a product to sell to every person in India that netted me just 50 cents each, I would make $500,000,000. I am still trying to think of that idea!

Tip #9: Be Decisive

"Be decisive and make lots of decisions."
Anthony Robbins

"Decisiveness is a characteristic of high-performing men and women. Almost any decision is better than no decision at all."
Brian Tracy

These are great quotes. You might be fantastic at business or investments, or writing or creating art, or whatever. But if you never make the decision to really go for it, you will never know if you could be successful, and the world will be worse off for it. Make a decision today and go for it!

Tip #10: Persevere

They say that if it was easy, everyone would do it. You will come up against barriers and frustrations and doubts and nay-sayers. But you have to keep persevering until the breakthrough happens. After a year in my recruitment business, I made a loss and I hadn't made one really lucrative placement. Things were not looking good and I was running out of money. I almost applied for a full time job. I went as far as downloading the job application form. I sat on the form for a couple of weeks, and I made a big effort to find a teacher for a vacancy I had in England. After lots of emails and phone calls I finally made my first big placement. That gave me the confidence (and some cash) to keep going. Within six months I was making a good profit, and I was on my way.

Tip #11: Win-Win

If you go into business, make sure your business provides a win-win situation for you and your customers. Many people have the mistaken idea that business is about screwing your customers or putting one past them. Nothing could be further from the truth. The more your customers win, the more they will tell others and the more they will come back.

Take a simple example. When you go to a shop to buy milk, you win because you don't have to own your own cow, or drive to a farm to get milk. The shop wins because they make a few cents on the purchase.

My recruitment company was a good example. When I placed a teacher, the teacher won because they found a good job, the school won because they found a good teacher, and I won because I receive a fee for the placement. It was a win-win-win situation.

Tip #12: Meet a Need

If you go into business you must meet somebody's need. People will love to do business with you because you meet their needs. Perhaps their need is more time in their day. If you offer them a fast efficient way of doing something for them, they will use your business.

If you see a need that is not being met, start a business to meet that need. People will flock to you to meet their needs.

Look at any successful business – a need is being met.

Tip #13: Work Smart, not Necessarily Work Hard

There is nothing wrong with working hard, and at some times in business you will need to work hard. However this should be the exception not the rule. If you work too hard "in" your business, you will not have time to work "on" your business. For example looking at strategies for growth, looking at trends in your business, or looking at what your competitors are doing.

One of the reasons for starting your own business is lifestyle. If you work too hard, you cannot enjoy a good lifestyle. Further, if you work too hard you can get too stressed and busy and tired to follow up on new opportunities and "great deals".

Tip #14: Be Entrepreneurial

Entrepreneurs either do something new or provide a new way of doing something that is already being done. Ignore most of what you have learned from text books and go out and break new ground, and make plenty of mistakes. The more decisive you are and the more mistakes you make, the more you learn and the more successful you will become.

Tip #15: Be Generous

I can't emphasize enough how few people practice this amazing technique. But it is hugely effective!

One excellent example is when I applied for some shares in an initial public offering (IPO) through my stock broker. The shares were very "hot" and were expected to stag (open strongly). The shares did in fact do very well, they went up 40% on the day they listed. I made $6,000 on one day. I was very pleased, and I rang a top restaurant and paid for a $150 voucher which I then posted to my broker with a thank you note. He had been broking for over ten years, and he told me he had never received a gift! Six months later another "hot" IPO came up. Guess who got the highest allocation of shares of all his company's clients? I did, even though I am a small client.

Another example is when a British Head Teacher flew out to interview a number of our teachers. He interviewed teachers at the local airport because he only had one day in the country. I phoned one of the restaurants at the airport and gave them my credit card number. I said the Head teacher could spend what he liked on dinner, and to give him a nice bottle of wine. I then told the Head Teacher the arrangement. He of course was delighted to have a free dinner during a day of interviews and was happy to take a nice bottle of wine with him. The total bill was less than $100. Soon after, we became that school's preferred supplier, and we earned tens of thousands of dollars in fees from them.

I cannot emphasize this tip enough times. Whatever you spend in being generous in business will come back to you tens or hundreds of times over. Of course that is not the main motivation. It is simply being a good human being to be generous to those around you. It also makes the world a better place to live.

Try it today! Send your 10 best customers or clients a real gift they will appreciate. Don't wait for it to be a Christmas gift. Just tell them you appreciate them!

Tip #16: Successful People help other Successful People

This is an amazingly powerful success tip. Successful people help each other to become more successful. Wealthy people help other wealthy people to become wealthier. Fit people help other fit people to get fitter. And so on.

If you want to be successful, help other people to become more successful. Don't charge people, give your advice for free. The reason is simple - those successful people will help you in return. It will also build your reputation and build goodwill around you. There are tons of successful people you can help with your skill base.

Let me give you a simple example. Say you have great internet skills. There will be a huge number of leaders or gurus in a field you are passionate about that do not have those skills or the time to learn. If you contact them and offer to set them up on all of the social media sites for free, and explain the benefits, they are likely to accept, and they will then want to help you! If you call them two months later and congratulate them on the new internet presence they have and then ask them if you can interview them for a teleconference, they won't refuse. You then have something of value you can use to raise your profile and give you social proof.

Chapter 63 - Quick Tips for a Better Lifestyle

Here are ten quick tips on achieving a better Lifestyle. These are easy to apply and enable fast and in often cases immediate Lifestyle benefits.

Tip #1: Accountability

Making yourself accountable to another person or a group is a very powerful way to ensure you do what you intend to do, and don't do what you know you are not supposed to do.

Let me give you a couple of examples:

At the beginning of 2009 in my trading business, I had a list of money management (risk) rules. However when a market looked especially attractive, I would deliberately break these risk rules I had set for myself. After a situation when this backfired badly I thought to myself "This is ridiculous. I have written down risk rules, and I don't follow them!"

So I emailed two people David and David who I have a huge amount of respect for and told them I needed two people I would be accountable to. I sent them my risk rules in full and committed to keeping to them. It has worked brilliantly.

The second example relates to this book. You need a lot of discipline to research, write, edit, rewrite, and format a book. It was taking me a long time to do everything, and some days I wouldn't get a chance to write. I decided to commit to my accountability group that I would write for at least an hour and a half every weekday. Of course my days are filled with my trading business, the work I do for charities, exercise, family, seminars etc. But after I made this commitment, my writing became a priority. On a number of nights I had to stay up late to make sure I kept to my commitment, but it worked really well, and I made much more progress than before.

Action Step 20:

If you have areas of your life you need to change or improve, find one or two people you have huge respect for, and would never like to let down and make a commitment to them. Remember they don't need to do anything except read your email. It is you who register in your mind that you have made a commitment, and you dare not break that commitment.

Also you can make a commitment to me! Yes, I am willing to keep you accountable. Here is how.

Make your commitment on the following webpage:

www.LifestyleBook.com/my-commitment

This is a confidential commitment between you and me. Your commitment must include a date. I will email you on your commitment date to confirm.

Please note: This is a real commitment. By committing, you are giving me permission to **kick your butt** if you do not follow through. Please do not commit unless you are willing to put everything else aside to make your commitment come to pass.

Tip #2: Stay in Motion

When I was a teenager, I heard a great analogy that has stayed with me. If you try to move a stationary car it is very difficult. You would need at least ten people to lift it up and move it. However if the car is already in motion, you only need to apply a small amount of turning pressure with one finger to the steering wheel and the car will move where you want it to go.

Human beings are just the same. If you are standing still, not going anywhere, in a rut, not making real progress it is very difficult for you to move or be moved towards something better. But if you are doing lots of productive things, always moving and always progressing, you will find that doors open for you, and you will begin to gravitate towards what really inspires you and really excites you.

I heard a good saying recently, "If you are going through hell don't make camp there, keep moving!"

Tip #3: Incremental Change

You do not have to make huge upheavals in your life in order to effect change. Let me give you an example from geometry. Say you need to travel 1,000 miles (or kilometers) in a straight line towards a city where there is a fantastic treasure. Either side of your destination is an alligator infested swamp. If your compass is out by just one degree (one three hundred and sixtieth of a full circle), do you know how many miles (kilometers) you would be away from the treasure once you had travelled the 1,000 miles (kilometers)? Over seventeen miles (kilometers). Plenty enough for you to be eaten by hungry alligators! Just by making a tiny incremental change (1/360th) you can radically change your destination.

The good news is that in your life you can start making incremental changes that will have hugely positive changes in your final destination. Simple examples include watching less TV, reading more, exercising more, eating healthier.

Action Step 21:

Commit to making just one incremental change in your life each month for the next three months.

Tip #4: Never be Late

Do you know the one reason people arrive late? They leave late. What I mean is; it is not the traffic, it is not the directions, it is not the last minute phone call, it is simply that they left late. In my experience most people arrive for business appointments late. In my industry (financial markets and fund management) we have a number of people visit for business meetings. Often they come with proposals or to ask us for to invest with them. It amazes me how many of them are late.

Being late tells me a few things about people:

They don't respect my time;
They are disorganized;
They are not someone I can rely on to keep a commitment.

Is this how you come across? If so, let it be the "you" of the past.

I have a strategy for never being late for a business appointment. I always allow a lot more time than I need and I always arrive early. I will often arrive 20 minutes early so I can find exactly where the meeting is, what floor it is on, etc. Then I will read a book or have a walk around the area. Remember a business meeting is a commitment. Never be late.

Tip #5: Buy Quality not Quantity

Always buy quality. This is even more important if you are on a budget. Quality feels great and looks great, and it lasts. A good example is clothing. Let's say you have a $400 budget for business shirts. It is far better to buy two $200 shirts than six $70 shirts. You will feel terrific, you will look amazing. You will notice, and others will notice. This principle is especially important if the expenses are related to your appearance, or the appearance of your business (business cards, stationery, website). But it is a principle that should extend to every area of your life.

Tip #6: Surround Yourself

Surround yourself with the best mentors, leaders, successes and minds in the world. You may not be able to meet them all personally, but you can get their books, listen to their speeches, watch their videos, or attend their seminars.

Tip #7: You Can't Manufacture Time

You can always make more money, but you can never make more time. Time is the most precious asset you have. Too many people trade their valuable time for a bit more money. That is a mistake. Enjoy what you have and enjoy it with those you love. Once this hour, this day, this week, this month is gone, it is gone forever.

Tip #8: Time Tips

As you can imagine, I am very conscious of preserving my most important asset. Here are some practical tips:

- Sometimes I get to take my kids to a kid's movie. That's great but it is not a good use of my time.

So I take a good book and sit right outside the cinema while they watch the movie. I just gained two hours.

- I always have a motivational or instructional audio-book in my car. While I drive I am learning.

- If I know I might have to wait somewhere I always take a book with me – dentist, doctor, bus stop etc.

- Unless I particularly want to have a one on one catch up, I try to organize ways in which I can catch up with a number of friends or business contacts at one time for example at a breakfast. This enables me to keep important friendships and contacts, but not spend hours and hours doing so.

- I often just say no. I evaluate invitations and opportunities. If they are not a really good use of my time, I politely decline.

- I put some things off until they need to be done. This might sound like procrastination but it really isn't. If I have a tax return due in on Friday, I will put it off until Friday. Then I really have to do it and I have to do it fast. If I start it on Tuesday I know I can take my time on it.

- For tasks that I know are going to require serious concentration, I ensure I do them in the most productive time in the day for me (mornings). That way I get them done fast.

When I am really tired and don't feel like doing much at all, I find a really simple task that needs to be done but doesn't need much brain power (for example getting a haircut).

Tip #9: Look Ahead

The faster you go, the further ahead you have to look. When you are walking slowly you can afford to look just in front of you. If you are running you have to look further ahead. If you are galloping on a horse you have to look further again. If you are in a racing car you have to look a long way forward. If you are in a jet aircraft you have to look many miles (or kilometers) ahead.

Your life is just the same. If you are slowly drifting along you don't have to look far ahead. But if you are speeding along achieving and growing at a fast rate, you have to look a long way ahead. You have to set goals and plan months and years in advance. Once you start speeding up your rate of change, remember to look up and look ahead.

Tip #10: Identify Key Areas of Your Life

We all have areas of our lives that are not satisfactory. You need to identify the main issues, isolate them and do something about them. Being decisive in this will have a huge positive impact in your life. To begin with just pick the biggest one or two issues and deal with them fast and clinically.

Chapter 64 - New Retirement

Retirement is one of the most disempowering words in the English language. It conjures up the image of someone who has worked long brutal hours for tiresome year after tiresome year with an annual three week "vacation". Then when society deems they are no longer at full productive capacity they stop doing what they have an ingrained habit of doing, and they "retire" on far less income than they are used to. Not only that, most people have to trust the government to top up their savings in order to give them a decent standard of living.

Leaving the standard of living of my retirement to a group of future politicians is not my idea of certainty and peace of mind!

Now I believe in being youthful for as long as possible. But the idea of a three month surfing vacation with my kids now is much more appealing to me than watching my grandchildren surfing when I'm in my seventies. Just like you I want to retire now, not when I'm getting old!

That is one of the things I loved about Tim Ferriss' book "The 4 Hour Work Week". He recommends restructuring your life so you can take "mini retirements" now. Work two months then take a month off. Work for a year then take six months off and backpack around the world for six months. Completely restructure your life so you earn passive or near passive income by only working a few hours a week from anywhere in the world.

Ferriss' book also makes the excellent point that most people actually don't want to be millionaires. What they really want is to be able to experience the lifestyle activities we think millionaires enjoy – time freedom, boating on the Mediterranean, diving the Great Barrier Reef from a boat you have chartered, having a full-time chef for a month. All these are possible if you live smart and think globally. If you are ready for a lifestyle change, I thoroughly recommend his book.

Another wonderful advantage of re-ordering your life towards running your own business in line with your passions is that you never have to retire! You can keep on managing your business and your life until they take you away in a box!

Imagine your life from next year onwards as a series of adventures or missions or experiences interspersed with periods of earning money doing something you love. That is the way I live my life, and there is nothing stopping you doing the same.

"Retiring early" can also be a trap. If you decide to work super-hard from the time you finish your education until you "retire" at 45 you have made a big mistake. First, you force yourself to work long hours and endure stress. Second, you will ignore far more important pursuits such as friends, family, spirituality and exercise. Third, you lose some of your most creative, energetic and productive years. Fourth, you are establishing a bad work habit that will be hard to shake off later. Fifth, once you reach 45 and "retire" what will you do all day, play golf and catch up on all the movies you missed? You would be bored within a month. Believe me, I tried something similar once.

I decided to have a six month retreat and just play my guitar and read the Bible. The first day I did a few hours of each, a few days later a bit less a week later a lot less, a month later I was sleeping 12 hours a day, I had no motivation, no energy, no drive, no direction. I played no guitar, didn't read my Bible, felt miserable and did basically nothing – it was horrible.

Human beings are designed to have habits and structures. My point is you need to develop great habits and structures now so the rest of your life is balanced. Live your life as you want to live it but keep structure, discipline and good habits.

Most of us take far too little vacation time. In February 2001 the World Tourism Organization reported that Americans took only an average of 13 days annual vacation, the fewest in the industrialized world. Further they reported:

- 34% of respondents said their jobs were so pressing they had no down time at work;
- 32% work and eat lunch at the same time;
- 32% do not leave the building during the working day;
- 19% said their job makes them feel older than they are;
- 17% said work caused them to lose sleep at home.

This is people in the wealthiest nation on earth! What is wrong with this picture?

Don't fall into the trap of thinking you will work hard for 30 years and then retire early. This is a lose-lose situation! You work too hard and miss out on 30 years of life and when you stop, you have too much time and no reason to get up in the morning. It is far better to plan your life so you make the most of each year by building in mini-retirements as well as regular fun, creative, spiritual, community and family-centered times.

Action Step 22:

Start now and plan one mini-retirement in the next six months (cannot include usual annual vacations).

Action Step 23:

Schedule vacation time now. Block out special days (anniversary, friend's birthday, long weekend away) on your calendar, and if you are employed, apply for a vacation day immediately. If you schedule it now, it will happen!

Chapter 65 - Before You Die Read This!

If you intend to live life abundantly and achieve your Perfect Lifestyle, you definitely do not want to have regrets at the end of your life. But the unfortunate fact is many people at the end of their life have serious regrets about what they did, and in some cases more importantly what they did not do. The purpose of this chapter is to learn from people who have end of life regrets to ensure we do not make the same mistakes and have the same regrets.

Researchers who have studied and interviewed people at the end of their life report eight common regrets:

1. Did Not Take a Leap of Faith

Many people at the end of their life look back at missed opportunities. A few times in every person's life opportunities and possibilities arise that require just a bit of courage, just a simple leap of faith. Don't be one of those people who look back and regret a conservative life always taking the "safe" option, or the "easy" path or the one with the most economic security. Life is short and life is for living – go for it when an opportunity arises! Start that business, take that overseas position, go on that wild expedition, write that book, buy that car you always wanted, lease your house for a year and backpack around the world!

2. Did Not Have the Courage to Live a Life True to Myself

When a person's life is almost over it is easy for them to look back and see how many of their dreams have not been fulfilled. A large number of people die knowing that due to choices they made in their life, they have not achieved their dreams. Too many people lived the life others expected of them.

From the moment you lose your health, it is too late. Health gives you a freedom very few people recognize until they no longer have it.

Live your life true to yourself. Live your dreams. Do what you really want to do.

3. Worked Too Hard

A huge number of people deeply regret spending so much of their lives working, like the proverbial rat on a wheel. So many people miss their children's best years, their spouse's companionship, opportunities they should have taken, and adventures they should have enjoyed.

We have all heard the stories of people on their deathbed. No-one ever says "I wished I spent more time at work." Or "Bring me my latest bank balance. I was to see it one last time." Or "Show me photos of my big boat and my cars." Yet so many people live their lives as if these are the most important things.

This book has given you the tools to ensure you can create a lifestyle that does not require you to work too hard, but rather to create a balanced life.

4. Did Not Have the Courage to Express how I Really Felt

At the end of their lives a lot of people are disappointed they did not have the courage to really say how they felt. Often people did not express their true feelings because they didn't want to cause trouble or "rock the boat".

However in being honest, relationships become more healthy and open. And it is better that people who don't like the "real you" move out of your life.

We need to make a point of saying how we really feel and being straight with the people around us.

5. Did Not Say what I Needed to Say

It is sometimes difficult to say what we really feel. How often do we tell the people we love that we love them? How often do we speak out our appreciation, gratitude, thanks? Many people deeply regret not saying what they wanted to and needed to say. Often the person concerned dies, and it is then too late.

About five years ago after I had my children, I realized how much love, kindness, sacrifice and effort my parents had given me when I was growing up. I wrote them a five page letter telling them how much I appreciated all of what they did to make my childhood the wonderful memory it is.

Action Step 24:

If this has prompted you or reminded you of someone you need to say something to, pick up the phone or write them a letter **now**. Don't let your lack of communication be a regret for you at the end of your life.

6. Did Not Forgive

Some people's biggest regret at the end of their life was not forgiving another person. Forgiveness is so powerful that a lack of forgiveness has been scientifically linked with large numbers of physical and psychological illnesses. It is important to remember that forgiving someone is not the same as saying what they did was right or acceptable. Rather it is releasing that person from your anger and hurt. If possible you can tell someone you forgive them, otherwise you can simply forgive them in your heart.

It is also a spiritual principle Jesus taught.

For if you forgive men when they sin against you, your heavenly Father will also forgive you. But if you do not forgive men their sins, your Father will not forgive your sins.
Matthew 6 v 14

Holding resentment against someone is similarly self-damaging. I like what Nelson Mandela said after being imprisoned for 27 years:

"Resentment is like drinking poison and then hoping it will kill your enemies."

7. Did Not Stay in Touch with Friends

Friendship is the spice of life. Some people's lives are so busy they neglect to keep in touch with friends. Everyone needs friends but perhaps never more than in old age and when a person is dying. Of course by then it is often too late to re-establish a friendship of 10, 20, or 30 years ago. In the final days and weeks of a person's life love and relationships are what matter.

8. Did Not let Myself be Happier

Happiness, joy and laughter are choices! Don't take yourself seriously. Don't try to be someone you are not for the benefit of those around you. Do what you love to do, be a free spirit, allow yourself to do crazy, memorable, wild things.

9. Did Not Live a Life of Faith

Connection with God is a key part of an abundant life. Census data shows that around 92% of people believe in God. However, few people actually make it a priority to seek and connect with God. You may have read these verses:

"You will seek me and find me when you seek me with all your heart."
Jeremiah 29 v 13

and

"God rewards those who diligently seek Him."
Hebrews 11 v 6

People at the end of their life often regretted what they knew to be important – a life of faith. Seek God now and do not neglect your spiritual life.

Action Step 25:

In *the next week* do something fun you will remember doing on your deathbed.

It doesn't have to cost anything. Perhaps get up at 4am and drive somewhere beautiful and eat three packs of strawberries while watching a sunrise. Even better, take a friend you are on the verge of losing contact with. Oh and tell them how you feel about them, and tell them something about the "real you" they don't already know. That would help to remove three regrets in one action. Perhaps take the day off work too, that would be four!

If you have read the wonderful book "Tuesdays with Morrie" by Mitch Albom you will remember that when Morrie knew he was dying, he said there were only four things in life that really mattered:

- Family
- Friends
- Community
- Spirituality

My hope is that we all make these four the main focus of our lives.

I also hope you:

- Take a leap of faith at every opportunity.
- Have the courage to live a life true to yourself.
- Work less.
- Have the courage to express how you really feel.
- Say what you need to say to the ones you love.
- Forgive everyone who has wronged or hurt you.
- Stay in touch with your friends.
- Choose happiness, joy and laughter.
- Seek and connect with God.

God bless you as you *Create* your Perfect Lifestyle.

Oli Hille
oli.lifestyle@gmail.com
(Please email me any questions or feedback.)

PS...

I have over 100 "**5 star**" reviews on Amazon for the Ebook version of this book.

If you enjoyed this book, I would REALLY appreciate you putting up a one or two sentence review on Amazon.

Simply go to www.Amazon.com/dp/047321508X

Click where it says "xx customer reviews", then click the button "Create your own review".

Thank you!

25% Discount Code

As a thank you for reading my book, you can order copies of this book for yourself, friends or family members and get a **25% discount!**

Go to this page: www.CreateSpace.com/3988149

Click the "Add to Cart" button:

\-   then simply enter this code into the discount box:

LMZVRZAB

Change a Life!

If you said to yourself "I wish I had read this book when I was at school or college." - take a minute right now to buy a copy of this book for someone you know who is at school or college. You can make a huge difference in a young person's life today.

Monthly Coaching Program

Now you have read the book, I encourage you to enroll in my Monthly Coaching Program.

Reading the book is only the first part. You now need to start creating your Perfect Lifestyle by **DOING**.

The monthly coaching program is designed to take you through every step of planning, setting goals and achieving your Perfect Lifestyle.

The program includes regular exercises, videos, tips, ideas, articles, challenges and so on to keep you on track. You will be mentored, encouraged and challenged to get the most out of life.

For more information on the coaching program visit:

www.LifestyleBook.com/coaching

Further Reading

If you enjoyed this book, check out my upcoming books:

1. "Creating the Perfect Trade"

A book about trading the financial markets. My average annual return on capital in the four years 2007 to 2011 was 58.78%. I disclose how I did it and the lessons I have learned in 20 years of trading the financial markets.

To sign up for launch updates go to:

www.TradingBook.net/launch

2. "Creating Property Wealth"

As the title suggests, a book about Residential Rental Properties. I outline how I got set up financially early in life by investing in Real Estate, and the lessons I've learned from 20 years of owning residential investment properties.

To sign up for launch updates go to:

www.LifestyleBook.com/links

3. "The Simulan Game"

My action adventure novel. I am in discussions with an academy award nominated Hollywood director re the screenplay:

To sign up for launch updates go to:

www.TheSimulanGame.com

Summary of Critical Principles

Critical Principle 1: The best return on your time (ever) will be the time you spend setting goals.

Critical Principle 2: You are the average of the five people you spend most of your time with.

Critical Principle 3: Children are the best thing in the world.

Critical Principle 4: Compounding your wealth is the most effective way to get rich slowly.

Critical Principle 5: Everything you own now will either be rust or dust or be owned by someone else in 100 years time.

Critical Principle 6: If you are not growing, you are dying.

Critical Principle 7: You need to find your true purpose in life and devote yourself to that.

Critical Principle 8: Continual failure is required for personal growth and development.

Critical Principle 9: Perseverance is the mother of achievement.

Critical Principle 10:   Words are far more powerful than we have been taught to believe.

Critical Principle 11:   Your body is a temple. Treat it as such.

Critical Principle 12:   Sometimes the best investment decision you make is not to invest.

Critical Principle 13:   Your chronological age is completely irrelevant to everything.

Summary of Action Steps

Action Step 1:

Read back over your answers to the Questionnaire in Chapter 1 and make notes on thoughts that have come to mind while you completed the questionnaire. If it has been a long time since you thought about the direction of your life, these thoughts and ideas will be invaluable in the weeks to come.

Action Step 2:

On a blank piece of paper write a list of everything you are passionate about, every interest, and every hobby. Don't think about business ideas, just write things down.

Action Step 3:

Identify one area of your life in which you need a high level peer. Identify two people who can be that peer. In the next 24 hours, make one simple step to start modeling that person. For example order a book they have written or contact them.

Action Step 4:

Systematically examine your monthly expenses. Go through your bank statements and credit card bills. Try to cut your expenses by 20%.

Action Step 5:

If you do not already volunteer and serve others, find a way you can use what you have to help someone else - at your church or community, a short term trip overseas, at a school or old person's home, with a charity or for a person in need.

Believe it or not it will benefit you more than them.

Action Step 6:

Set aside ten minutes in your day where you will be alone, quiet and undisturbed. Get up early in the morning if you have to.

Sit cross legged on the floor with you back to a wall. Close your eyes and start taking slow and deep breaths, breathing in through your nose and out through your mouth. Your tummy should be rising and falling while you breathe, not your chest.

Now imagine you are in an empty house except for the furniture, and you are looking out at a view of the ocean. Spend five minute right there looking out to sea. After five minutes of peacefully clearing your mind of any other distraction, ask yourself these questions:

What is my purpose in life?
How can I make the world a better place?
Where would I feel the most contentment and fulfillment?

Do this will no pre-conceived ideas and just allow your heart (and God if you are a believer) to tell you the answers to these questions.

Write down whatever you feel. It might be just a snippet, or a thought or an idea, or a picture or a plan.

Action Step 7:

Make a list of the characteristics of the Future You. Start modelling as many of these characteristics as you can.

Action Step 8:

Complete these steps (a) to (e) with a piece of paper. Take action today!

Remember some of the decisions you make will be mistakes, but that is okay. Mistakes are simply learning experiences. We need to allow ourselves to make mistakes and we need to allow ourselves to fail.

(a)   Identify Your Goal

Ask yourself where you want to be in five years. For example with my dream partner, in a job/business I love, in my own debt free house, with a published novel!

(b)   Admit Your Fears

Until you admit your fears specifically you cannot address them. For example "I fear the unknown and failure if I completely change my career path."

(c)   Consequences

Concentrate on what your life will be like if you **don't** change, and emphasise how bad it will be! For example: "If I don't change I will be stuck in this dead end job until they make me redundant and then I'll be unemployable and I'll be broke and I'll also die lonely because I haven't got the guts to ask out the person I like!"

The more you focus on the negatives of **not** changing, the more you will be motivated to change.

(d)   Identify Areas for Change

Specifically identify areas of your life you are not happy with that need change. Write them down.

(e)   Be Decisive

Don't prolong the pain! Make a decision right now i.e. today! Planning your next five years starts right now. Write that resignation letter now, phone the person you want to ask out right now! Whatever it is, start the process now.

If you are still having trouble making a decision go back to step (c) and tell yourself over and over how much worse your life is going to be if you stay in your rut.

Action Step 9:

Think about an area of your life where you keep doing the same thing over and over but it is not working.

It is time to do less of that or stop it altogether and find another approach.

Think about an area of your life where what you are doing is producing excellent results. Try to find ways to do that activity more and more, and also apply that activity to other areas of your life.

Take a blank piece of paper and write down one area of your life where you know this principle applies. Write down ways that you can do more of what is working and/or less of what is not working.

Action Step 10:

Try something NEW in the *next 24 hours*, and if you fail, embrace it then move on.

Action Step 11:

Write down the three limiting beliefs that have been holding you back the most. Under each one, write down the negative consequences you have already experienced through holding each belief.

Then on a separate piece of paper write each limiting belief with a space under each one. Now write down an opposite empowering belief for each. Then most important, cross out the limiting belief.

For example:

~~"No matter what I do I'll always be overweight."~~

"I can be slender and gorgeous!"

~~"The best result I can get is a bit above average."~~

"I can achieve excellence if I put my mind to it!"

~~"I am no good at relationships; I may as well be single."~~

"I love people, people love me and I'm going to be the perfect partner for someone!"

Close your eyes and see yourself actually cutting those limiting beliefs out of your mind and putting them in a blender and blending them. Then pour them into your sink and see them get washed away.

Write your three new empowering beliefs on a new piece of paper and read them aloud to yourself every day with energy and enthusiasm. I have used this technique myself and it really works.

Action Step 12:

Take a blank piece of paper and write down on the left side all of the limiting mental barriers you either speak or think.

Once you have done that, write a corresponding positive statement that over-writes and replaces your mental barrier.

Some examples:

"~~I could never afford that.~~"

"How could I afford that?"

"~~I feel sick and tired.~~"

"I'm healthy and fit and I don't get sick."

"~~I couldn't start a business.~~"

"I'd be very successful in business."

"~~I could never be that good.~~"

"I excel at everything I work hard at."

"~~I'm not good enough to get that job.~~"

"I am able to succeed at whatever job I do."

You can literally re-program or re-socialize your mind by repeating the positive statement and developing the habit of thinking and speaking positively. This effectively breaks down any limiting mental barriers.

Action Step 13:

Write out ten positive and affirming self-statements and repeat them five times each day. In three minutes a day you will (over time) transform your attitude, your behavior and your reality. Have you ever met someone who was determined to achieve something? Someone whose determination propelled them past others who were more naturally gifted? Determination is simply the physical outworking of self talk statements such as "I will succeed" "I will never give up" "I'm going to make it no matter what gets in my way".

Action Step 14:

Write down your five minute meditation and starting tomorrow; begin to create your own day.

We can eradicate negative thoughts and by doing that, help to create a day that becomes more positive, creative, loving, effective, and therefore more life-changing.

One of the main attributes of our humanity is we can change who we are, what we feel, what we believe and what we achieve. The start of that process is changing our thoughts and attitudes from negative ones that suck life out of us to positive ones that lift us up and recharge us.

Once you start directing your day from the start and taking control of how you think about yourself and what is happening to you, you will find you can actually shape your day and even create your day. Wouldn't that be a wonderful way to live!

Action Step 15:

Pick the one habit or situation you want to change and go through each of these steps:

1. Give yourself leverage
2. Make a mind-shift
3. Make a decision
4. Take action NOW
5. Set a Goal
6. Create a habit

Action Step 16:

Always keep business cards and email addresses and websites of friends, acquaintances and casual contacts.

Action Step 17:

Next week make three specific changes in the amount you move. Arrange a walk, take some forced breaks, and walk up stairs instead of taking the elevator.

Action Step 18:

Next week set aside just five minutes a day to just sit in a quiet place on the floor, back straight and legs crossed (chairs and couches are too comfortable, this is not a power nap!), and breathe, listen, wait, meditate, and pray.

Action Step 19:

Commit to yourself and one other person that you will take three small steps every day towards fulfilling your dream.

Action Step 20:

If you have areas of your life you need to change or improve, find one or two people you have huge respect for, and would never like to let down, and make a commitment to them. Remember they don't need to do anything except read your email. It is you who register in your mind you have made a commitment and you dare not break that commitment.

Action Step 21:

Commit to making just one incremental change in your life each month for the next three months.

Action Step 22:

Start now and plan one mini-retirement in the next six months (cannot include usual annual vacations).

Action Step 23:

Schedule vacation time now. Block out special days (anniversary, friend's birthday, long weekend away) on your calendar and if you are employed, apply for a vacation day immediately. If you schedule it now, it will happen!

Action Step 24:

It is sometimes difficult to say what we really feel. How often do we tell the people we love that we love them?

How often do we speak out our appreciation, gratitude, thanks? Many people deeply regret not saying what they wanted to and needed to say. Often the person concerned dies and it is then too late.

If this has prompted you or reminded you of someone you need to say something to, pick up the phone or write them a letter **now**. Don't let your lack of communication be a regret for you at the end of your life.

Action Step 25:

In *the next week* do something fun you will remember doing on your deathbed.

"How to Become an Amazon #1 Bestselling Author – and Make Money!"

Ebook by Oli Hille

If you have a desire to write a book and make money from selling it, this is the book for you.

I spent over $5,000 on courses and books and training, plus six months studying how Amazon works so that I could launch my first book. My first book became an Amazon #1 Bestseller because of the knowledge I had gained.

This book is over 100 pages long and gives step by step strategies that almost no-one knows about. You can purchase the Ebook here:

www.LifestyleBook.com/amazon

"Amazon #1 Bestselling author, Oli Hille, is a true master and authority on what it takes to succeed in the new world e-publishing. He has a proven track record and I found his information and expertise invaluable in helping to get my own book to #1 on Amazon."
Richard Kelley, Author and MD

"Little did I know, that by employing his strategies I would hit #1 within 11 hours."
Anna Morrison, BSN, RN, CLNC – Author

"Oli helped me get my first book to #1 Amazon Bestseller Status, by providing inspiration, easily applicable practical tips and continual support during the launch."
Lori Webb, Author

Free Webinar for Authors

I recorded a 1 hour and 48 minute webinar for authors who want to know how to publish a book on Amazon Kindle. Thousands of people have watched it.

You can view it here:

www.YouTube.com/watch?v=Zt4spXkpG8U

"Science Fiction Short Stories"

Ebook by Oli Hille – just 99 cents on Amazon!

This is a 37 page book that contains four Science Fiction short stories.

1. "Birthdaysuit Case"
What happens when an ordinary man is mysteriously shaped into a suitcase? And why do the CIA get involved?

2. "The Price of Pain"
What is the alien spaceship doing inside earth's atmosphere? And what are they searching for?

3. "Love Nest"
Why does Albert leave work soon after being bitten by a strange varmint? And why doesn't he leave his house?

4. "Run Time"
What happens when the lines between reality and virtual reality get blurred?

Also Included - Free Bonus: Chapter 1 of my upcoming novel "The Simulan Game"

You can purchase the Ebook here for 99 cents:

www.Amazon.com/dp/B00727UJQO

"The Price of Pain" alone is worth the full cost of the book. All four tales are captivating, well written, and full of wonderful imagery. Truly delightful reading."
Emily Moore

"The Simulan Game"

A novel by Oli Hille

The United Nations has risen to be the only world superpower. Its rule has brought global peace to the earth for the first time in centuries. But beneath the surface is the underclass who continue to be denied the rights and luxuries of the elite. Franco emerges from the underclass and becomes one of the elite. But under the polished veneer is a boy from the underclass who wants to change the world.

For information on purchasing please visit:

www.TheSimulanGame.com

"Creating the Perfect Lifestyle" is now available in Spanish.

Get the Spanish Ebook here:

www.Amazon.com/dp/B00AHO9CBW

Order another copy now:

Email orders: orders@LifestyleBook.com

Postal Orders: Empire Publishing
                   PO Box 17599
                   Christchurch
                   New Zealand 8081

Please send me _____ copy (copies) of
"Creating the Perfect Lifestyle". I understand
that I can return any of them for a full refund -
for any reason, no questions asked.

Name: _____

Address: _____

City: _____

Country: _____

Post Code: _____

Email: _____

Copies are $29.95 plus $5 P&P.

For bulk orders email:
orders@LifestyleBook.com